"This book is the first that addresses the symptoms and the impact of codependence in nursing. The disease is driven by the very essence of nursing, which requires that patients receive constant attention and where the actions and treatment of professional peers often deny the nurses sense of self-worth. I highly recommend this book to any nurse."

> Breathline
> American Society of Post-Anesthesia Nurses

"This book is excellent. While the challenge is great, the opportunities for change are many. What a relief it is to be told we now can make positive choices for ourselves, both personally and professionally. The 'core issues' (of codependence) can be addressed and we can treat the disease instead of quick fixes for the outward symptoms of the nursing shortage, burnout, and stress-related illness."

> Advancing CLINICAL CARE Journal
> National Organization for the Advancement of Associate Degree Nursing

"This is a 'must read' book for all nurses, from administrators to students. It provides basic knowledge of codependence and specific strategies for change, both personally and professionally. A required reading text for all."

> Patricia O'Brien, RN,CAC
> Project Coordinator-Peer Assistance
> New Jersey Nurses' Association

"This book takes a hard look at the profession of nursing and its interdependence with the nurses' home life and self-concept. The main focus is the relationship between codependence and nursing. It is well-written, interesting, and informative."

> Maine Nurse
> Maine Nurses' Association Newsletter

"This book is based on real situations, faced by real nurses who have come to recognize the codependence within themselves and their entire profession. The book provides a look at the core issues of the disease and offers practical and encouraging suggestions for beginning a personal and professional journey toward wellness."

> Beginnings
> American Holistic Nurses' Association

I'm Dying to Take Care of You

Nurses and Codependence
Breaking the Cycles

by Candace Snow and David Willard, R.N.

FIRST EDITION, 1989

ISBN: 0922352-01-1
Library of Congress Catalog Card Number 89-063131

Cover Design by Technigraphic Systems, Inc., Edmonds, WA

DEDICATION

This book is dedicated to our children
Faith Snow, Jesse Snow, and Patrick Rayne-Willard

In the hope that the gifts of recovery
may be channeled through us to you
and through you to all children
everywhere

ACKNOWLEDGEMENTS

We wish to acknowledge our parents—Ford and Claudia Harbaugh, Fran and Bill Willard—who were challenged in their parenting of these spirited children who entered their lives; Candace's brother, Max, and sister, Denise, who introduced her to her love of mothering as she cared for them; David's brother, Thom, who introduced him to brotherhood. Our love and gratitude to you all for continuing to love, support, and encourage us even when you didn't understand.

We acknowledge our extended family of friends today—the women and men who care for us each day—too many to list, but you know who you are.

We acknowledge our teachers: Keith McKee, Corabelle Swanston, Marcia Smith, Pia Mellody, Lloyd Parker, Tim Franklin, Brian Bouch, Earl Herr, Nancy Feinstein, Lee Jampolsky, and Ken and Mary Richardson. Each of you led us through a crucial part of our recoveries, and you continue to be loved and appreciated for your integrity, inspiration, example, and guidance.

We acknowledge Sharon and Ed Hearn, Cliff Creager, Bonnie Elson, and the staff at A/D Communications Corporation. Thank you for believing in us, for respectfully challenging us to create a more cohesive manuscript.

We acknowledge our colleagues in nursing who, through their vision and sense of possibility, supported us in writing this book.

Finally, we acknowledge our family. We give our thanks: To one another for the love, tenderness, constancy, acceptance, nurture, and passion—we never dreamed we could be so blessed. To Faith, our daughter, who has been always forgiving, always loving, always honest; whose integrity and wisdom we admire; who has given us pure, unadulterated joy. To Jesse, our son, whose brilliance and courage astound us; whose humor delights us; who taught Candace patience and faith as they struggled together for his survival. To Patrick, our son, whose acceptance, love, creativity, and sweetness touch us deeply, bringing us all closer to our Child Within.

FOREWORD

This book suggests a new way of thinking about some of the problems faced by the nursing profession and its members. Codependence is the underlying concept. Codependence, as defined by the authors, is a disease induced by child abuse (anything that shames a child) that leads to self-defeating relationships.

How does codependence evolve? What are its symptoms? Is codependence prevalent in nurses? What is the evidence? What is the effect upon nurses as caregivers? What is the impact of codependence upon the development of nursing? What can be done about it? These are the questions addressed in an open, engaging manner by Candace Snow and David Willard—wife and husband, parents, caregivers, and codependence sufferers.

"I'm Dying to Take Care of You" opens with a personal invitation to examine how you feel about your life and talks about ways to make it better. From this personal level, the book then proceeds to lay a foundation for further development of theory and research on codependence and the nursing profession. The scope of recovery outlined begins with individual self-assessment and therapy and broadens to encompass institutional and professional problem-solving around issues of codependence.

Tracing our problems as adults and as a maturing profession to childhood experiences and developing solutions around this evolving symptomatology will be difficult for most of us. Indifference, incredulity, and pain may compete in our range of emotions as we read on.

Candace and David compel us to ask the critical questions, and, most important, to envision the possibilities for change.

Margretta M. Styles, R.N., Ed.D., F.A.A.N.
Livingston Professor of Nursing
University of California San Francisco

INTRODUCTION

The information in this book is offered primarily from an experiential base. Though certain theoretical perspectives are integrated, much of this book shares what we have learned and experienced, and the gifts we have received in our recovery and through participation in the recovery processes of others.

Those astute in psychological theory may find this information difficult to accept. We can only respond to such a reaction as we always have: This work and the practices associated with it have been profoundly impactful in our lives and in the lives of others. It makes a difference. It is helpful. Therapists working from these suggestions find them invaluable. We believe in this work and want to share our beliefs and understanding in treating codependence with nurses—and with those who help them.

We view the nursing profession with tremendous respect, gratitude, and compassion. We recognize the brilliance, the courage, the physical, emotional and spiritual stamina, the caring, the creativity, and the base of knowledge that the men and women of nursing bring to the profession. We also recognize the lack of appreciation, the abuse, the discounting, the unrealistic demands they experience in their personal lives and in their nursing practices.

It is our hope that this book begins and continues a process of healing for nurses as individuals and collectively for the profession of nursing. We hope that nurses will take this information and apply it to their lives and work.

If this book is to have a singular impact, it is our hope it will be in drawing us together in a sense of fellowship in nursing, working *together* to bring the profession back into balance, placing the focus where it was intended: on nurses as ministers of healing for themselves and others.

Candace Snow
David Willard, R.N., C.D., C.A.C.
Carmel Valley, California

TABLE OF CONTENTS

> *All the strong things of her heart*
> *came out in her body,*
> *that had been tireless*
> *in serving generous emotions.*
> —**Willa Cather**

I

NURSES AS CAREGIVERS

All six gurneys are occupied, and the waiting room is jammed. Two nurses race from bed to bed, ministering to patients in this busy metropolitan emergency department. The department physician stands behind the desk at the nurses' station, speaking with the attending physician in the emergency department at a nearby hospital. He arranges for the transfer of the patient on bed two, whom he suspects has a closed head injury. Four patients are ready to be seen; one patient awaits a consultant to review his stabilizing episode of supraventricular tachycardia.

People in the waiting room fidget impatiently. The air is tense with anger ("Why isn't someone attending to my son's cut chin?"), fear ("Is my husband having a heart attack? Will he be all right?"), pain ("Nurse, is that guy ever going to give me something for this headache?"), shame (The police enter the room with a handcuffed, intoxicated middle-aged man screaming sexual obscenities). It's a routine evening in the emergency department in this city of 75,000.

The consultant arrives, demanding to see the

1

EKG and progress notes, neither of which can be found. One nurse turns and says, "Check the counter behind bed one," to which the physician replies, "Come find it for me!" In icy silence, the nurse leaves her patient and rummages through the mess on the counter. Shame, anger, and fear have been dumped into the environment. The second nurse presses the emergency department physician to hang up the phone and see the child with the lacerated chin. The unit secretary, who was walking through when the consultant arrived, reenters the room and slams charts in the rack with the charts of other patients waiting to be seen. She looks furious, and when asked what's wrong she says, "Nothing!" She spends the remainder of the shift swimming in resentment. Later she is found in the break room on the phone, telling her husband she has to find another place to work.

When the house supervisor enters right about now, asking, "How's it going?" she receives an incident report shoved in her direction. The entire "family"—nurses, unit secretary, emergency department physician, nurse manager, consultant, and patients—has taken on and is acting out the shame, anger, and fear that really belong to one physician and an intoxicated patient.

Replayed, this scenario could have sounded like this: "I'm not able to get there to help you look right now, but when you get a minute, let's talk." Whether time or willingness would allow, clearing the way for straight talk would give this nurse the opportunity to maintain her integrity while giving her a moment to remember that the physician's shameless behavior is not about her. His anger, sarcasm, shame, and fear are more about him. The shameless behavior and shaming messages of an intoxicated patient are not about anyone in the environment other than himself. Quite often, in the heat of a busy clinical setting, nurses are willing to say nothing, soaking up everyone's feelings like a sponge. In the above scenario, an agitated, inappropriate colleague and an intoxicated patient were enough to stir the "family" into emotional chaos.

Acting accountably to the nurse's statement, "Let's talk when you get a minute," the consultant could have said, "Sorry I snapped. I've had a busy one today and have a lot on my mind."

Codependence in nursing
Caring about the welfare of others is the foundation of nursing as a spiritual discipline. Nursing is also a physical, social, biological, and behavioral science. Blending the theoretical and practical ideas from these disciplines into nursing practices that promote care of self in proportion to the care given to others is an art. Codependence draws us off balance into caring for others at the expense of ourselves, creating professional disillusionment and personal pain—anything but an inspiring practice. Our experience indicates that codependence creates harmful consequences for better than 80 percent of the nursing profession.

Codependence emerges as a learned set of behaviors exhibited by children raised in dysfunctional families. It leads us to esteem ourselves by what we do, what we look like, or what we have, rather than by who we are. As nurses, it invites us to give away our power as a spiritual body of women and men to the perceived abusiveness of an unwieldy medical bu-

3

reaucracy; and to addictions, eating disorders, unhappy primary relationships, burnout, and physical and mental illness.

The issues of codependence translate to the practice setting in a variety of ways. They are seen as symptoms of the primary problem—which *is* codependence—but are manifest as arrogance, grandiosity, people-pleasing, tolerating the abusive behavior of others just to keep them liking us, and using walls of anger, fear, or shame for our personal boundaries. These inappropriate boundaries can make us appear unempathetic—or appear to have no boundaries at all, which leads to picking up and carrying the pain or feelings of others, thus losing a sense of our true gifts in the healing process. Further, in relation to our own wants and needs, codependence leads us to wear the mask of being needless and antidependent—or, to the other extreme of being too needy and too dependent. It leads us either to wear the mask of superhood or to appear chaotic and unsafe as caregivers.

Lastly, and perhaps most importantly, as the result of professional expectations and the issues we bring to the profession from our families, nurses often adopt a mask of being controlled and perfect. When we do this, the essence of true healing—an accepting connection with the body, mind, and spirit of a patient—is blocked. Instead, we come to believe that healing is possible only through conformity with the treatment plans we write, and that perfection is an attainable goal—one we must be able to reach despite the cost to ourselves and others.

One of our most difficult decisions when we began working with nurses and issues of professional codependence was this: We acknowledged, through our own recovery from codependence, that personal issues of codependence translate directly to the practice setting in very understandable ways. Anyone talking about these issues has to get "bone honest" about choices they have made. How do we begin, we wondered, to address the issues of codependence in the face of the shame, fear, anger, or pain it might create? We know that to educate others about codependence, two things have to happen. We have to invite people simultaneously to *get excited* about recovery and to *start hurting* over the price they continue to pay for their unresolved issues of codependence.

Given the authors' relational, sexual, emotional, and addictive histories, it is not surprising that we fit together like a hand in a glove. Each of us has been married more than once. In succeeding relationships we repeated similar dysfunctional patterns, thinking we were doing something different, only to awaken to the realization we had done the same things in different ways. Each of us works in a helping profession. Each has used a variety of chemicals to sedate the feeling and thinking we carry as a legacy of our family experience. Each of us has acted out of the pain, shame, fear, and certainly anger at knowing something inside was wrong, while feeling powerless to control or change that mysterious "something." Each of us has experienced tremendous difficulty with intimacy. When first together, we each had problems knowing what we needed, wanted, thought, and felt. We each used behaviors we weren't aware of, and we certainly had difficulty with straightforward, clear communication as a result.

There is no easy way. Personal recovery from codependence challenges us to examine our lives without minimizing, denying, or deluding ourselves into thinking that everything's okay. So, too, recovery from professional issues of codependence—issues that affect the practice of nursing at the deepest levels— must be guided by our willingness to confront lovingly our minimization, denial, and delusion about what nursing has become.

It is our deep belief that whether codependence is a trendy word of the eighties, soon to pass for something else, or a real phenomenon that once again allows us the opportunity to work at achieving a lasting sense of inner peace, its manifestations do exist. Codependence is a constellation of dysfunctional thoughts, feelings, behaviors, and attitudes that effectively prevent nurses from engaging in the inspired work that is their art.

During the past decade, research from the fields of psychology, medicine, sociology, and addiction treatment; and data from the movement to help adult children of alcoholics, have provided clearer understandings of the disease of codependence. Frequently, the word "codependence" has been associated with those individuals raised in families where alcoholism exists. It is clear, however, from the recent work of Charles Whitfield, Timmen Cermak, Robert Ackerman, Pia Mellody, John Bradshaw, Anne Wilson Schaef[1,2,3,4,5,6] and others, that the phenomenon of codependence can exist, develop in, and emerge from circumstances in families where alcoholism is not present.

It is the purpose of this book to explore and expand on the work of others and to set forth what we believe are reasonable suppositions about codependence in the nursing profession, laying groundwork for personal and professional recovery and for further discussion and investigation.

Chapter I Reference Notes

[1]Charles Whitfield, "Co-Dependence: Our Most Common Addiction," *Wellness Associates Journal*, Spring 1988, pp.1-6.

[2]Timmen Cermak, *Diagnosing and Treating Co-Dependence* (Minneapolis: Johnson Institute Books, 1986).

[3]Robert Ackerman, *Children of Alcoholics: Bibliography and Resource Guide* (Deerfield Beach, Florida: Health Communications, Inc., 1987).

[4]Pia Mellody, *Facing Co-Dependence* (San Francisco: Harper & Row, 1989).

[5]John Bradshaw, *Bradshaw On: The Family* and *Healing the Shame That Binds You* (Deerfield Beach: Health Communications, Inc., 1986 and 1988).

[6]Anne Wilson Schaef, *Co-Dependence: Misunderstood—Mistreated* (San Francisco: Harper & Row, 1986).

*A great many people think they are thinking
when they are merely rearranging
their prejudices.*
—William James

II

THINKING ABOUT CODEPENDENCE

Over the past three decades, we have worked in the helping professions in a variety of capacities. Our work has taken us into hospitals, clinics, therapy sessions, childcare study centers, parenting organizations, teaching settings, religious practices, nonreligious practices, days with the homeless, and ultimately through the beginnings of our own journeys into recovery from the diseases of addiction and codependence.

As we made progress in our recovery processes, we began working with others, reading their work, and appreciating their struggle with the enormity of and confusion about the origins of addictive processes and this word "codependence." About three years ago, we had the good fortune to train with Pia Mellody, whose work in making sense of the confusion about addictive processes opened the door for us into viewing codependence more clearly.

At the time, both of us worked in the recovery profession as counselors and educators. We were struck by the similarities between the symptomatology of relapse in the disease of alcoholism and other

9

drug addictions, the behavioral symptomatology of the "dry drunk" syndrome (exhibiting the emotional and spiritual symptoms of alcoholism without drinking), and the symptomatology of untreated codependence. Could it be, we posited, that we're really talking about root issues, which, when sifted through, indicate that these symptoms are very closely related or, in truth, are parts of one and the same phenomenon?

As our investigation into addiction and codependence continued, coupled with our continued path in recovery, we explored our personal issues. We became more aware of the issues of dysfunctionality that existed in our own family—with our children and with our families-of-origin. Still working in the health care industry, we became more aware of elements of dysfunction in the industry that seemed to mirror our perceptions in our family—lending credence to Anne Wilson Schaef's and others' beliefs that organizational health reflects the level of health we bring into the workplace.

Many authors have noted that a large number of nurses are adult children of alcoholics. Some have estimated that better than 80 percent of helping professionals were raised in "dysfunctional" families. Schaef[1] challenges us to think about our health care organizations—indeed *most* organizations—as dysfunctional families.

Nurses have been studied for years on issues of low or nonexistent self-esteem, burnout, stress and stress-related illness, not having time to spend with patients, and the disparity between the altruistic ideals purported in training and the realities they perceive in their practice places. Almost universally, nurses have been the target, and the subject, of numerous studies to determine why they leave the profession.[2] Indeed, in the United States there is a shortage of nurses by about 30 percent in relation to the demand for their services—despite the fact that the number of nurses licensed to practice who were actually practicing nursing rose from 77 percent in 1980 to 80 percent in 1986.[3] It also is clear that fewer college students want to enter nursing, wages are compressed (if not stagnant), and enrollments in nursing programs have declined precipitously.[4]

One nurse recently described the events that cemented her decision to leave nursing. She cared for a terminally ill young man on her unit. At the end of her shift, she usually stopped in his room to talk. They had developed a bond that was including her in his process of dying—a privilege, she told us. Believing her practice was one of healing mind, body, and spirit, she felt this part of her work day was appropriate and rewarding. During one particularly hectic shift, she received a message that he needed to talk with her. His condition was deteriorating rapidly, and she tried all during her shift to get to his room. Her shift extended into overtime, and she left the hospital thoroughly exhausted both physically and spiritually, promising herself she would arrive early the next day to spend time with him. She was greeted by the sight of his stripped mattress the next morning. Unable to face one more experience that prioritized "paper over people," she resigned.

Codependence and nursing

Eventually, our work focused on issues of codependence and nursing. There has been much, over the years, to push nurses away from the profession: a sense of being underappreciated, assault by the inappropriate behavior of others, divisions and confusion arising from nurses sensing that something is wrong with the profession (and if only the administration would get it together, everything would be okay), wages not increasing commensurate with other professions over time ... the litany of grievances is endless.

There also is the awareness that something is very right about nursing. The profession offers nurses an opportunity to define, and practice from, their own spiritual beliefs about healing. At its best, nursing provides a safe, loving environment in which healing can occur; it embraces an expansive understanding of healing through research, clinical practice, and the integration of spiritual principles.

Charles Whitfield's definition of spirituality seems applicable to nursing: a practice that "is subtle, yet powerful, and therefore paradoxical. It is personal, practical, and experiential ... that is, you can *feel* it. It is inclusive, supportive, and nurturing, and yet transcends the psychological and physical realms of experience."[5]

Three years ago, when we were jarred by the notion that the dry drunk syndrome, the relapse dynamic, and untreated codependence incorporated common symptomatology, and we coupled that awareness with our experience of nurses as they struggled with a profession that embraces such paradox, we arrived at an interesting hypothesis. Our thoughts were: The issues of codependence (or, as Schaef believes, the addictive process) lead to relapse and blocked progress in recovery, while working on these issues leads to healing. Also, we believe that 75-90 percent of nurses bring unresolved issues of codependence from their families-of-origin into their practices in pain-filled, overwhelming environments. Is it possible, therefore, that burnout, certain elements of the nursing shortage, professional malaise, and addictions to chemicals, food, sex, and unhealthy relationships are related largely to nurses hiding their codependence issues under the veil of loving and caring for others? Our experience leads us to believe it is more than possible—it is quite likely true.

To see codependence as it really is

We have watched with interest and compassion those who have contributed to the expanding literature that seeks to understand and define codependence. Codependence has been examined by theorists in the fields of counseling, family therapy, psychiatry, addiction treatment, medicine, mental health, and religion.[6,7,8,9] To "treat" or understand a clinical phenomenon, our society wants causes and cures.

Struggling for a working definition of codependence has led to interesting results. Anne Wilson Schaef, an incisive writer and psychotherapist, summarizes many commonly used definitions in her 1986 work, "Co-Dependence: Misunderstood—Mistreated."[10] In examining each definition, she notes that most evolved with a missing link, primarily as a result of the perspective of the author. Some authors failed to include etiologies outside the framework of the dysfunctional family; others excluded codependence from families or groups unless alcoholism or chemical addiction existed. Still others associated codependence with psychiatric diagnoses and failed to see the relevance of advancing therapies or strategies for a phenomenon they believed was already well enough understood and treated.

Schaef believes codependence is a disease, as do many others, and takes the view that codependence is a subdisease under a more generic designation: "addictive process." Whitfield, she notes, formerly excluded codependence from groups that did not include an alcoholic or addict, and yet he was one of the first thinkers to expand the influence of codependence to institutions, political bodies, and nations.[11]

Whitfield views codependence as "a general and pervasive part of the human condition such that it *is a category under which many, if not most, conditions can be subsumed.*"[12] He further notes that one of the disadvantages of viewing codependence as a distinct diagnostic entity (as Schaef suggests, a subdisease of the addictive process) is that, in so doing, it may lose its power as a general and pervasive dynamic of the painful side of our humanity.[13] The common symptomatology of codependence has been described in the "Diagnostic and Statistical Manual of the American Psychiatric Association" in many ways: anxiety disorder, compulsive personality disorder, mixed personality disorder (now called personality disorder not otherwise specified), post traumatic stress disorder, dependent personality disorder, and dysthymic disorder.[14]

Whitfield further defines codependence as "our most common addiction" and a "disease of lost selfhood."[15] We believe this is the clearest, simplest definition we have read; yet, from our perspective, we do not believe it says enough. Having been trained by Pia Mellody in 1986 to work with the educational components of the disease of codependence, we began to

14

recognize the validity of her premise that codependence has a direct connection to abusive or shaming experiences in childhood.

Why all this prelude to our definition? Because we know our definition turns heads. Since we have experienced our own recovery processes and have worked with hundreds of others struggling with their own issues of codependence, we feel it is useless to mince words. We believe that recovery invites self-honesty, acceptance, and a developing spirituality. We believe that recovery invites us to grieve, to challenge ourselves biochemically as well as spiritually, to confront every outside fix we use to sedate our realities. We believe that until we confront the issues of the shaming process, which is the fundamental legacy of abuse that drives the disease of codependence, we give lip service to recovery processes generally and continue to raise a nation of children whose realities are rooted in fear, anger, shame, and pain— children who will grow up to perpetuate the abuse of others and themselves in every relationship at every level.

We believe, as do Whitfield, Bradshaw, Mellody, and others, that codependence is the overriding phenomenon driving children to relate to themselves and others in inappropriate ways in adulthood. It is the same phenomenon that prevents us from recognizing the profound impact of the disease of addiction on our development as a nation!

Our definition, then, is that *codependence is a disease induced by child abuse, that leads to self-defeating relationships with the self and others.* This definition contains some words that threaten; cause us to throw up defenses like minimization, denial, and delusion; and make us say, "That doesn't apply to me." Saying that codependence is a disease of lost selfhood may make looking at the process more palatable.

Codependence is a disease

When we say disease, we mean *disease*. Some like to view codependence as a "state of dis-ease," but that softens the impact and too easily allows us to defend our thinking with minimization, denial, or delusion. The best descriptions of the characteristics of disease come from the chemical dependence treatment literature.[16]

A disease is *primary*. This means the symptoms are not caused by something else. *Codependence is the primary problem*. When we are hustling around on a busy medical unit and a particularly demanding patient takes most of our time to the exclusion of care we might have provided to other patients during the shift, we might feel shame. If we know we have given our attention appropriately and understand we are not perfect, we can be willing to be held accountable by other patients, a manager, or a colleague. We might be able to problem-solve ways of doing something differently the next time without dropping into feelings of worthlessness, hopelessness, or despair. If, on the other hand, we leave the shift and feel unworthy, worthless, or emotionally overwhelmed—like we should have been able to do more—the cause of the problem is not the demanding patient, understaffing, or a dysfunctional profession. The cause of the problem is the disease of codependence. Our tendency is to place the cause for our inner conflict outside the self, to say it's caused by something else.

Codependence is *progressive.* Simply put, untreated or without recovery, codependence gets worse over time. If you had checked in with David at the age of 15, for example, you would have seen a young man who tried to gain self-esteem by "doing." David acted out his family pain by covering it up with accomplishments. Candace, on the other hand, acted out her family pain and sense of hopelessness through deep depression, a serious suicide attempt, and making only passing grades. Checking in with both of us at age 38, you would have found us much sicker; our combined symptomatology included numerous unhappy primary relationships, addiction to various chemicals (including alcohol), and addiction to various self-defeating behaviors.

Professionally, as a registered nurse, David continued his caretaking role and kept recovery at a distance by caring for the wants and needs of others. He could hold up his accomplishments whenever anyone said, "God, you must be lonely," and would "do more" to prove to himself that everything was okay. Candace esteemed herself by living through and for her children. Always working, she had serial "careers" (none particularly successful), was anorexic and depressed, and felt hopeless.

It was not until we both got into recovery, first from our addictions and then from our codependence, that our lives began to stabilize. The progression of the disease was then arrested.

Codependence in its middle and late stages ultimately progresses to levels of physical and mental illness. Regardless of whether chemical addiction exists, codependence is an etiological agent for depression, acute and chronic gastric disorders, genito-urinary disturbances, respiratory disease, heart disease, suicide, battering, and rage attacks leading to heinous crimes against women, homosexuals, people of color, and the poor.

Codependence is *chronic*. Simply put, codependence doesn't go away. As with alcoholism, once you've got it, you've got it. There is no pill, no therapy, no 28-day treatment program that will make codependence go away. In the jargon of the trade, you can be "in your disease" in seconds, and although there are therapeutic and personal strategies you can employ to abate the symptoms, codependence, like diabetes, is permanent.

Codependence is *fatal*. It is not obvious in the early stages of the disease how something as seemingly innocuous as codependence can kill you. We doubt there has ever been a death certificate that read, "Cause of death: Codependence." What we see more commonly are such diagnoses as heart failure, alcoholism, drug overdose, suicide, depression, hemorrhagic ulcerative colitis, gunshot wound to the chest, intracerebral hemorrhage, or something similar.

The developing field of psychoneuroimmunology has recently quantified something we have known intuitively for a long time. That is, nonendogenous, noncognitive stressors can cause illness.[17] The biochemical changes that occur in the immune response as a result of undergoing continued shaming, carrying the induced realities of others, watching or listening to abuse, being shamed for being needy, and receiving the litany of exogenous stimuli that a dysfunctional boundary system allows into our psyche, *lead to quantifiable physiologic changes that can lead to early death.* In training, we learn from "biopsycho-social" models of clinical thought. In codependence, we face our deepest "biopsychosocioculturospiritual" roots.

In his book, "Everything I Needed to Know I Learned in Kindergarten,"[18] Robert Fulgham describes a tribe in the Solomon Islands who have a fascinating ritual with trees too large to be felled with an ax. If a tree is too large to be dropped with tools, the men in the tribe encircle the tree, screaming at it morning and evening for 30 days. At the end of the 30-day period, it is told, the tree would die and fall over. The natives believe the screaming kills the spirit of the tree. The same is true of human beings; repetitive abuse "kills the spirit" and biologically sets our chemistry in motion to create the constellation of disorders associated with codependence.

This disease is *treatable.* Thus far we have described a disease as primary (codependence is the problem—the symptoms are not caused by something else); progressive (codependence gets worse over time); chronic (codependence doesn't go away); and fatal (codependence takes lives in a variety of serious and painful ways). The good news is that codependence is treatable. There may or may not be a locus on a chromosome that predetermines each person's endowment for codependence. But either way, by working to resolve the issues of codependence at their roots, each of us can do our best to complement our genetic heritage. We can live happier, healthier, more hope-filled lives.

Codependence is induced
By induced we mean literally "shot into." We are

assuming that a child comes onto the planet with a well-mapped, but not well-understood, genetic endowment in relation to the issues of codependence. That is, there may be data indicating that certain proteins code for the characteristics that predispose us to codependence, but they haven't yet been delineated. So, while geneticists work on this, we will assume that a child is essentially "blank" at birth, capable of being influenced profoundly by the environment.

When we are born, we have the capacity to feel anger, physical and emotional pain, fear, and shame. We refer you to Gershen Kaufmann,[19] John Bradshaw,[20] and Pia Mellody[21] for more thorough discussions on the origin and nature of shame. Children also are not able to discriminate between someone else's irresponsible behavior and their own behavior. When we say *induced*, we are saying that a parent or caregiver who acts irresponsibly with any part of their feelings, thinking, or behavior, literally shoots their reality into the child's feelings. When a husband rages at his spouse, shame, anger, fear, and pain are induced into his listening children. When a baby is not held, shame and fear are induced.

Since children cannot intellectually drop a boundary in place to protect themselves from the definitions of others, part of the package that develops in any part of their reality (thoughts, feelings, behavior, looks) does not belong to them. Children then carry others' reality around with them, and this carried or induced reality becomes the seed for a developing pool of shame. ***This induced reality is what drives the disease of codependence.***

Codependence is induced by child abuse

Most professionals have come to view child abuse as physical or sexual acts that invade the physical or sexual boundaries of a child. Indeed, the justice system still does not recognize emotional, social, or spiritual abuse. If it did, its calendars would overflow. Maya Angelou writes of the abused child: "... a child is born knowing nothing. The abused child learns to believe in nothing and hence grows to live out and experience the hopelessness of cynicism."[22] Codependence operates out of this "spiritual cynicism," this "believing in nothing." It is a most terrible legacy for a child—that question, "Is this all there is?"—and the subsequent hopelessness despite youth and supposed innocence. Whenever this sense of hopelessness toward oneself and life exists in a child, can we presume to say that what happened to that child was not abusive?

Had David not entered recovery, his sarcasm, rage, shame, and fear would have continued to be induced into his children. Had Candace not entered recovery, she would have continued saying nothing, at great personal sacrifice, to protect the children from David's out-of-control behavior. The children—carrying David's shame, fear, and anger, and Candace's pain, shame, and fear—avoided David and tried to "fix" Candace. Allowed to continue on this path, our children would have grown to experience problems with intimacy that would baffle them for years. How could we presume to say what happened to them was not abusive? Many nonrecovering families do precisely that. We hear, "Kids have to learn how to be tough. It's good for 'em." Consistently abused children grow hard, cynical, brittle. They lead empty emotional lives. More about this in Chapter VIII.

It is not enough to assume that child protection workers should be the ones to investigate and restrain individuals who emotionally, socially, or spiritually abuse their children. Child protection workers in most cities can barely manage the caseloads they have without adding something as intangible as spiritual abuse to their agendas. Yet repetitive episodes of spiritual abuse are just as shaming as incest or daily beatings. It is not enough to expect social service workers to stamp out child abuse. It is the responsibility of each of us to get real about what child abuse is and to begin talking about it in a straightforward manner!

Child abuse is anything that shames a child. A child who is beaten every day is shamed, and the outcome is obvious. A child who is overcontrolled every day by a narcissistic parent is shamed. If the shaming behavior continues, the outcome in either case is the same. Both children learn to focus on sources outside of themselves as ways of living happier lives—hoping, *believing*, that outside experiences are the only way to sedate the shame of their own experience. What we are saying is that the nature of the child's inner reality in either case is filled with shame, fear, anger, or pain that does not belong to that child. This induced reality is the legacy of abuse that drives the disease of codependence. Children are not codependent. Children exhibiting the symptomatology of codependence are abused children.

Codependence leads to self-defeating relationships with the self and others

Codependents learn to focus outside of the self for definitions of their safety, their value and well-being, their wants and needs, their connection with the universe. We learn as nurses to maintain "peace at any price" in our professional environments. We often defer our clinical contributions (thinking or skills) to the thoughts and healing practices of our colleagues because we don't believe our ideas have value. "Who would listen anyway?" or, "Nursing has been this way for a hundred and twenty-five years, and nothing's going to change now. Besides, I'm too close to retirement to make waves," are common self-defeating phrases we often hear from nurses. Talk about the hopelessness of cynicism!

For those of us who are codependent, what starts out as a focus outside the self, as Whitfield notes, must "ultimately become an inner search for wholeness and completion,"[23] if we are to *live* rather than merely *survive*. In our relationship with ourself, the abusive nature of our childhood leads us to invalidate, discount, and distort our history and to perpetuate the delusion that inner peace is attainable from the outside in. In our professional relationships, we focus on caring for others at the risk of great physical, emotional, and spiritual consequences. With friends and families, we choose relationships that are unfulfilling and empty, and that end in divorce, physical or sexual violence, or any combination thereof.

As parents, we may make a decision never to parent *our* children in the ways we were parented—and then do precisely that—or end up parenting our children from the other extreme: permissive, tolerant, engulfing, and smothering. We then wonder why our children struggle with intimacy and become addicted to chemicals and self-defeating behaviors. The abuse in either extreme is just as severe, and it results from parenting through the skewed thinking that accompanies codependence.

When David became a father, he overcontrolled nearly every element of his environment—children, appointments, lists of lists, how the furniture was arranged (or rearranged), how and when people did what and why. Candace was permissive, controlled her feelings, said "yes" when she meant "no," and was chaotic and disorganized. A painfully perfect fit in relationship. Both of us focused on our children and one another for the sole definition of our value and well-being.

Our families blended and "stabilized." Piles of baggage from other relationships filled our house with pain and confusion. David looked good to himself, angry to others. Candace looked and felt exhausted and stressed. Our children acted out our struggle—Faith, by being good; Jesse, with hostility and shame; Patrick, with blends of silence and school problems. Our personal and professional lives were vaporizing. Carrying the family pain into his nursing practice, David became resentful, burdened by its weight. Candace carried the pain of David, the children, *and* her clients. We needed help!

What is critical to understand about the self-defeating nature of codependence, both personally and professionally, is that no one else is going to fix us. Until we examine carefully whether we operate from an other-directed focus and see how that translates into our practice settings, little will change within us, and nothing will change within the profession. To give you an idea of what we're talking about, let's take a look in Chapter III at a nurse whose issues of codependence are easily identified.

Chapter II Reference Notes

[1]Anne Wilson Schaef, *The Addictive Organization* (San Francisco: Harper & Row, 1988), pp.77-137.

[2]Marlene Kramer, *Reality Shock: Why Nurses Leave Nursing* (St. Louis: C.V. Mosby, 1974).

[3]American Nurses' Association, "Defeating the RCT and Similar Proposals," American Nurses' Association, RCT 4, January 1989, pp. 1-19.

[4]California Nurses' Association, *Allocation of Nursing Resources: The Facts* (brochure compiled and published by the California Nurses' Association from: Secretary's Commission on Nursing, 1988; Hospital Fact Book, 1987; various publications from the California Nurses' Association and American Nurses' Association, 1988), pp. 1-4.

[5]Charles Whitfield, "Co-Dependence: Our Most Common Addiction," *Wellness Associates Journal*, Spring 1988, p.4.

[6]Matthew Fox, "Is the Catholic Church Today a Dysfunctional Family? A Pastoral Letter to Cardinal Ratzinger and the Whole Church," *Creation*, Nov./Dec. 1988, pp. 23-37.

[7]David Hilfiker, *Healing the Wounds: A Physician Looks At His Work* (New York: Viking Penguin, Inc., 1985), pp. 189-207.

[8]Sharon Wegscheider-Cruse, *Co-Dependency: An Emerging Issue* (Pompano Beach, Florida: Health Communications, Inc., 1984), pp. 1-3.

[9]Robert Subby, *Lost in the Shuffle* (Deerfield Beach, Florida: Health Communications Inc., 1987), pp. 21-26; 93-98.

[10]Anne Wilson Schaef, *Co-Dependence: Misunderstood—Mistreated* (San Francisco: Harper & Row, 1986), pp. 13-19.

[11]Ibid., p. 21.

[12]Whitfield, op. cit., p. 4.

[13]Ibid., p.4.

[14]Ibid., p. 4.

[15]Ibid., p. 1.

[16]Vernon Johnson, *Intervention: How to Help Someone Who Doesn't Want Help* (Minneapolis: Johnson Institute Books, 1986), pp. 5-9.

[17]Eric Smith, "Lymphocyte Production of Endorphins and Endorphin-Mediated Immunoregulatory Activity," *Journal of Immunology*, 135, (2), August 1988, p. 781s.

[18]Robert Fulgham, *All I Really Needed to Know I Learned in Kindergarten* (New York: Villard Books, 1986), pp. 19-20.

[19]Gershen Kaufman, *Shame: The Power of Caring*, Rev. ed. (Cambridge: Schenkmen Publishing Company, 1985).

[20]John Bradshaw, *Healing the Shame That Binds You* (Deerfield Beach: Health Communications, Inc., 1988).

[21]Pia Mellody, *Facing Co-Dependence* (San Francisco: Harper & Row, 1989).

[22]Maya Angelou, "That Which Lives After Us," In P. Woodruff and H. Wilmer (Eds.), *Facing Evil: Light at the Core of Darkness* (Peru, Illinois: Open Court Publishing Company, 1988), pp. 21-36.

[23]Whitfield, op. cit., p. 4.

What is strength
without a double share of wisdom?
Vast, unwieldy, burdensome, proudly secure,
yet liable to fall.
—John Milton

III

CLAIRE
A CASE HISTORY

Claire is a 37-year-old critical-care nurse working in a very busy 10-bed unit in a 100-bed district hospital. She has worked for the organization for 15 years and is respected by her colleagues. According to her performance evaluations, she has provided excellent care for her patients. For the past three years, Claire has been developing a teaching curriculum for post-infarction cardiac patients and their families and has implemented several modifications in the cardiac nursing protocols used in the ICCU.

Today, Claire is in recovery for codependence. A year ago, she lived alone and rarely left her apartment during off-work hours. Her supervisor had observed that she'd become sullen at work. She was 45 pounds over her ideal weight for height, seldom took breaks during her shift, and had been absent from work with upper respiratory infections an average of five days a month. She did not smoke at work but smoked cigarettes at home.

Her colleagues experienced her as moody, abrupt, and quiet most of the time, except for occasional outbursts of anger that usually were directed toward a nurse, physician, or other colleague. When confronted by the nurses closest to her about her moods, Claire usually justified her behavior by quoting a particular policy or procedure that a colleague failed to follow in providing care. Most of her issues with colleagues were directed at time . . . blood gases not drawn by the lab on time, meals not coming from dietary hot or on time, other nurses not on time for their shifts, patients not receiving medications on time, portable x-rays not taken by the time a physician arrived to read them.

Claire's nurse manager took her aside after one of her patients expired from cardiac arrest and asked her about the case. Claire's only comment was, "Well, if people around here knew what they were doing when a patient codes, we wouldn't lose so many. There's absolutely no reason this patient should have died. He didn't receive external massage for a full two minutes after the monitor went flat and the jerk physician intubated his esophagus!" With that, Claire stomped off and sat in the lounge.

The manager spoke with other members of the resuscitation team for their views of the situation. The patient, 64 and dying of congestive heart failure, had experienced several episodes of bradycardia during the night. He had been in intensive care for 11 days, comatose for the past three. When the cardiac monitor indicated asystole, five of Claire's colleagues were at the bedside within seconds. They began external compressions, intubated the trachea within one minute of arrest, and administered cardiotonic medications at appropriate times—all according to protocol. The patient died because his lungs were filled with fluid, and his course in ICCU had progressively deteriorated. The patient had fixed pupils and was areflexic. An electroencephalogram performed the day prior to death showed essentially no change from the day before: little activity, possible brain death.

Claire's supervisor went into the lounge and sat with her. Sullen, head down, shaking, Claire said, "I just can't do it anymore. I'm working with a bunch of incompetents!" Following her manager's careful explanation of the clinical features of the case, Claire quietly left the room and returned to work.

At work the following week, Claire spoke quietly, became more withdrawn, developed a cough. Two weeks later, she was diagnosed with acute bronchitis, was given antibiotics, and continued working. Without the weight gain and the history of frequent use of sick leave, one might view Claire's history as isolated, associated with the stress of working in critical care, and looking like she's just grumpy and needs a few days off.

The symptoms we saw in Claire's case, however, indicated issues of codependence: explosive feeling attacks, infrequent breaks, chronic sick time due to stress-related illness, and overweight. Claire's symptoms reflect the needlessness and antidependence often seen in nurses who function beautifully in the clinical arena but appear to need no one emotionally. These nurses often feel resentful of colleagues who take breaks or can ask for help when they need it. Eating disorders, sex addiction, or both frequently are part of the package. Claire believed the only way she could justify taking time off from work was to be sick. To ask for a "mental health day" was out of the question.

Claire used walls of anger and shame for boundaries. From this position, she was invulnerable, impenetrable, and perceived as aloof and unapproachable. When confronted by her colleagues, she protected her reality with anger—anger that frequently seemed out of proportion to the issues being discussed. In her patient care, Claire lowered her boundaries and became enmeshed with her patients; she had difficulty recognizing where she left off and they began.

In relation to issues of reality, Claire was controlled and perfect. She performed all her clinical tasks on time and to the letter, and was controlling of other nurses' care, often asking them to discuss their rationale for doing something in a particular way. For Claire, there was only one right way to accomplish nursing care. Her focus was almost entirely "other-directed." When her manager held her accountable for her behavior or examined clinical situations with her, Claire could not see her own behavior as a reflection of her inner process. She defended her behavior with theory, anger, or by pointing out someone else's clinical ineptitude.

From our perspective, though her colleagues perceived her as a nurse with excellent clinical judgment and skill, she was not very much fun to work with—emotionally unavailable, judgmental, controlling, needless, a supernurse. Behind the walls, behind the explosive feelings that resulted from her inability to ask for her needs to be met, behind the perfectionism and professional arrogance, was a woman in deep emotional and spiritual pain.

When Claire ultimately was hospitalized with

pneumonia, additional history was revealed. During her off hours, she cared for her dying father. Not even her closest friends knew her father was dying of cancer of the colon. Her reclusive mother had given over most of her husband's care to Claire. Three weeks prior to her admission to the hospital, Claire's older brother was jailed because of a hit-and-run drunk-driving charge. She exhausted her entire savings to fund his bail and attorney's fees.

As a nurse, Claire was an excellent practitioner though difficult to work with. As a woman, she was tremendously lonely, carrying and acting out the family pain in a variety of self-destructive ways. She practiced nursing from a perspective of arrogance, which masked her low self-esteem; and she used walls of anger and shame to protect her reality, often offending others with her thinking or feelings. She came to her work from a position of needlessness, masking her inability to care for herself physically and mentally, which prevented her from working interdependently with others. She wore the mask of superhood, an extreme that gave others the impression that she was rigid and supermature.

She tried to control the reality surrounding herself and her coworkers as well as the care her coworkers provided. At the same time, she would not allow her colleagues to hold her accountable for her behavior or to discuss their perceptions of her clinical work.

Claire's early recovery
Claire eventually was referred to us by a patient who overheard her discussing her brother's alcohol problems with another nurse. During the family intervention process, Claire finally saw the price she

was paying for preventing her brother and other members of her family from experiencing the consequences of their dysfunctional behavior. She began to focus on her own recovery from codependence.

Intervention with her brother was deferred due to the legal consequences of his drunk-driving charge, for which he ultimately was sent to prison. In a follow-up visit with the family, Claire announced to her mother and father that she could no longer assume Mom's role as primary caregiver for her dad, and that she would start attending Twelve Step meetings that focused on recovery from codependence.

Claire called us six months later to tell us she was continuing with Twelve Step program meetings and had begun seeing a therapist for assistance with her eating disorder. Though she still had tremendous difficulty knowing how to ask for help at work, still "exploded" now and then, and still got "knotted up with patients and their pain," she had begun to get honest about her pain. She felt better—better about herself, better about remaining in the profession.

Recovery is an odd process. The patient who overhead Claire talking to another nurse about her brother's hit-and-run drunk-driving charge was a client of ours whose wife—also a nurse—had committed suicide 10 years earlier.

Critical care nurses often are the most difficult to reach. They can easily hold up their accomplishments as a way of esteeming themselves, but will shield from view others' perceptions of their work, saying, "Listen, my private life is none of your business. You see something wrong with my care, tell me about it; otherwise, buzz off!" Nurses pay a tremendous personal and professional price for issues of codependence in their lives. Our most appropriate interventions with colleagues must be designed around learning to identify effectively and talk about these issues so that they can arrest the progression of the disease.

We define professional codependence as *any act or behavior that shames and does not support the value, vulnerability, interdependence, level of maturity, and accountability/spirituality of a nurse, colleague, or patient.* Professional issues of codependence are directly related to our level of personal health in each of these five areas—the "core issues" of codependence. The core issues emerge from five fundamental beliefs about children (Table 1, page 34).

A child begins life filled with value, extremely vulnerable, needy and dependent, immature, and imperfect. From these assumptions, the core issues evolve: issues of esteem, boundaries, dependency, moderation, and reality. A nurse presumably enters the profession with a clear sense of his or her value, capable of utilizing functional boundaries, capable of functioning interdependently, capable of living and practicing moderately, and capable of being held accountable for personal and clinical realities (Table 2, page 35). It is this presumption that has led researchers to study nurses from so many divergent perspectives and, paradoxically, thwarted their efforts to assist them.

Table 1. Evolution of Codependence

QUALITIES OF THE CHILD	THE DISEASE OF CODEPENDENCE		RECOVERY
Valuable	Grandiosity	Low Self-Esteem	Self-Esteeming
Vulnerable	Invulnerable	Too Vulnerable	Boundaries
Needy/ Dependent	Needless Antidependent	Too Needy Too Dependent	Interdependent
Immature	Supermature	Superimmature	Mature Within Age Level
Imperfect	Controlled Perfectionistic	Chaotic	Accountable Spiritual

Copyright 1986, Pia Mellody. Used with permission of the author. This chart has since been modified by Pia Mellody and appears in her book, *Facing Co-Dependence* (San Francisco: Harper & Row, 1989).

Table 2. Evolution of Codependence in Nursing

Relative percentages of nurses who, by self report, categorized their codependence issues utilizing the Codependence and Nursing Self-Assessment Inventory. Data explained in Chapter 4. (Adapted from the work of Pia Mellody, 1986.)

PRESUMED ENTRY-LEVEL QUALITIES	PROFESSIONAL CODEPENDENCE Those Having Issues in Both Extremes		RECOVERY
Aware of Own Value and the Value of Others	← 11% → 23% Superiority Grandiosity	60% Low Self-Esteem Professional Shame Issues	3% Self-Esteeming Emotionally Responsible With Self & Others
Appropriately Protective & Respectful of Self & Others	← 17% → 19% Rigid Inflexible Offender Issues	60% Carries Others' Realities Victimization Issues	4% Appropriate Boundaries
Appropriate With Needs & Wants	← 21% → 55% Needless Antidependent	16% Inappropriate With Needs & Wants	1% Interdependent
Mature Within Age Level	← 9% → 21% Superimmature Moderation Issues	38% Supermature Moderation Issues	1% Lives and Practices Moderately
Aware of Own Spirituality and the Evolving Spirituality of Others	99% Controlled Controlling Perfectionistic	Procrastinative Chaotic	1% Accountable Spiritual

*Let me listen to me
and not to them.*
—Gertrude Stein

IV

TAKING AN HONEST LOOK
AT NURSES

In November 1988, we conducted a computer search of the medical and nursing literature at the University of California, San Francisco. Of 813,000 citations, 1,400, or 0.02 percent, contained publications under the descriptors "addiction" and "chemical dependency." Fourteen of 813,000, or fewer than 0.00002 percent, cited articles on the addicted nurse. The International Nursing Index contained no citations about codependence and nursing. There were, however, over the past 15 years, several citations discussing issues of nurses and burnout, nurses and effective communication with colleagues, nurses and alcoholism, and nurses dealing with difficult people; as well as articles articulating the similarities, differences, and disparities between women and men in nursing on a variety of clinical and administrative issues.

As we began applying our understanding of codependence to nurses, speaking with nurses about their families-of-origin, and listening for the common dialogue that emerged from their concerns about the profession, we devised a self-assessment tool to measure five areas of interest. Compiled from a list of statements from our personal and professional experience, and from other sources,[1] our data revealed the following:

Of 139 nurses from five different areas of the United States who attended a seminar entitled, "I'm Dying To Take Care Of You—Codependence and the Nursing Profession,"* 138—or 99 percent—participated in the Codependence and Nursing Self-Assessment Inventory (Table 3, page 51). The inventory consists of 121 statements designed to help nurses identify issues of personal and professional codependence in five areas: esteem, boundaries, wants and needs (or dependency issues), moderation, and reality (physical reality, or what you look like; feeling reality, or what you feel; behavioral reality, or what you do and don't do; and thinking reality, or what you think or don't think). You may find it useful to examine your own issues of codependence with this instrument.

It is important to note that strict statistical treatment was not applied to the tool, nor was there a control group. Our intent was to begin evaluating nurses on what we believe are the core issues of codependence. We also wanted to provide them with a way of seeing where most of their codependency issues existed and, thus, where to begin working in recovery.

Because our data admittedly contains bias, we use it with caution. For example, we do not make the assumption that because individuals were raised in dysfunctional families they must, therefore, have unresolved issues of codependence. At the same time, to use data as a way of minimizing the impact of

*A six-cassette lecture series on Codependence and the Nursing Profession by Candace Snow and David Willard is available from Past Company, P.O. Box 1213, Carmel Valley, California 93924.

family dysfunction on a nurse's ability to function appropriately within the contexts of nursing is equally discounting. We view our initial attempt at this research as a search for the truth—and an invitation for others to gather more data. Decisions on the five core issues of interest were largely guided by and patterned after the work of Pia Mellody.[2] Mellody is a registered nurse whose pioneering work in understanding codependence makes the most sense to us.

Value

Our data showed that ninety-three percent of those responding have esteem issues. Sixty percent believe their self-esteem to be low and, professionally, wear the mask of people-pleasing. They esteem themselves by "doing," by tolerating the inappropriate behavior of others to be "liked," by believing that other nurses are more valuable to the organization than they are, by using chemicals, sex, or food to sedate their reality, or by overcommitting themselves. Essentially, they abandon themselves under the veil of caring for others.

Twenty-three percent of those responding to esteem issues indicate they adopt a mask of arrogance and grandiosity to cover their low self-esteem, appearing to themselves and others as rigid, contemptuous, judgmental, better than others, striving for power, alienating of others, or perfectionistic. In any case, the underlying issue is low self-esteem. Nurses pull on the "one-up, better-than-others" mask because feeling and living in the pain of worthlessness is too overwhelming.

Self-esteem, in the spiritual sense, is having a fundamental awareness of the presence of a Power greater than ourselves in our consciousness, knowing that we truly are whole, spiritual beings having a human experience. From the work of Jael Greenleaf[3] and others, it also is clear that self-esteem is a function of our deep personal awareness of our value— that we are valuable and valued for who we are, not because of what we do. From the work of Merle Fossum and Marilyn Mason, Pia Mellody, John Bradshaw, and others, it is clear that a functional family is capable of supporting the value of a child and gives children the verbal and nonverbal messages that they are extremely valuable, but no more and certainly no less so than anyone else in the family.

One expectation of the nursing profession, and indeed most helping professions, is that by the time you enter the practice *you are aware enough of your own value and have the capacity to lovingly support the value of others. Thus you know that, no matter what feelings or activities float around in the environment, your value as a nurse and as a human being is not at stake.*

Regardless of whether they were raised in families where addictions existed, less than three percent of the nurses evaluated believe or act in ways that reflect the belief that they are filled with value and valuable simply for who they are. Eleven percent of respondents have issues in both of the extremes, "Arrogance and Grandiosity," and "Low Self-Esteem." As a result of esteem issues, nurses are better able to support the value of others than their own.

Taken alone, as has been the case throughout the nursing literature, examining and posing solutions for why nurses have such low self-images is less than useful. Based upon the contributions of several authors writing from the perspective of recovery from addictive disease, and from our experience, self-esteem issues are merely a part of the package.

Protection and respect of self and others

Our self-assessment tool next examined the issues of internal and external boundaries. In a metaphysical sense, boundaries have been noted not to exist.[4] In a very real sense, however, boundaries are attitudes and beliefs—modeled for children by a functional family—that teach children to develop ways of protecting and respecting their physical, sexual, emotional, and spiritual limits and definitions. By extension, then, as adults, they are able to respect and protect the same in others.

Boundaries function to allow us a moment of choice to determine how we will be touched (by whom, when, and where); whether we will allow others to define us (our thinking, feeling, behavior, and how we look); and whether we are willing and capable of being held accountable when we offend others. With a healthy sense of our own boundaries, we are much more likely to enter the profession of nursing *knowing* when we are being abused in some part of our reality, and *knowing* when we are offending others.

Eighty-four percent of the nurses we polled have boundary issues. Sixty percent believe they function professionally with *no* boundaries. They tolerate the inappropriate behavior of others; carry patients' or colleagues' pain, shame, fear, or anger for them; have difficulty maintaining their own thinking; experience difficulty with intimate relationships; and often believe they are responsible for others' thinking, feelings, or behavior. Nineteen percent use walls of anger, fear, pain, or shame rather than functional boundaries. Seventeen percent have issues in both extremes—no boundaries and inappropriate boundaries.

Those nurses who use walls for boundaries are perceived by colleagues as unempathetic, unapproachable, distant, or aloof. Behind walls, the inner state is one of tremendous loneliness and emotional or spiritual pain. With no boundaries, caregivers are perceived as either superempathetic by patients or colleagues, or as too fragile or too weak to function in the often overwhelming, crisis-oriented environment of the health care system in this country.

Dependency issues
Ninety-three percent of the nurses responded to the items addressing issues of needs and wants. Fifty-five percent view themselves as needless and antidependent, 16 percent view themselves as too needy or too dependent, and 21 percent have issues in both extremes. A mere *one percent* feel they function interdependently!

Mellody,[5] Richardson and Munroe,[6] and others describe *needs* as those elements of living that we perceive as necessary to survival or to physical and emotional development. They include: food, clothing, shelter, emotional nurturing (the need for time, attention, and direction from another), physical nurturing (the need for other than sexual touch from another, such as walking close together, being held, hugs), and, in our culture, medical and dental attention. Everything else is a want or preference. Depending on your perspective, some wants may be perceived as needs, but those listed above are the only ones we will consider "needs" for the purposes of this discussion.

Dependency issues emerge from the assumption that a child must receive adequate nurturing for needs *and* learn from caregivers how to ask for needs and wants to be met. A functional family does this for a child.

In a dysfunctional family, however, issues of codependence emerge in the adult child as the result of being shamed for being needy, or being given the message—either verbally or nonverbally—that they are capable of taking care of the wants and needs of others and *should* want to do that selflessly, to the exclusion of their own needs and wants.

For nurses, it is expected that they enter the profession well on the path to self-actualization; that is, they are capable of functioning interdependently and should leave their needs and wants "at the door" and "be there" for the wants and needs of patients and their families.

For nurses who enter the profession needless and antidependent (the most desirable type of employee in the eyes of most health care organizations), common symptoms include: frequent urinary tract infections due to not taking time to rest, take fluids, or even to urinate when the body says "urinate"; anorexia, bulimia, bulimarexia, and compulsive over- or undereating due to inappropriate attention to the need for food; and pain or resentment from watching others have needs met while their own needs go unattended.

At the other extreme, nurses all too frequently get their needs met indirectly by taking care of the wants and needs of others. They commonly feel too needy or too dependent. As a result of the shame they feel for being needy in an environment that says "Don't be needy," nurses frequently become addicted to food, sex, alcohol, drugs, serial unhappy relationships, and work—and feel powerless to stop. The resulting physical and mental illness provides a way for nurses to feel they have a bonafide reason for taking time off from work, leading to increased pressure on the employer to fill in in their absence, increased insurance costs, and increased costs of patient care.

Chronic, hidden depression probably is the greatest single mental illness that nurses report to us—primarily, we believe, due to a sense of hopelessness over giving away personal power by taking care of the wants and needs of others at the expense of their own needs for food, rest, time, attention, and direction from colleagues. These therapeutic ingredients are just as necessary for nurses on the job as they are for their patients.

Not surprisingly, many nurses find that their symptoms of depression clear as they work a recovery program for their unresolved issues of codependence. Many nurses recovering from the disease of chemical addiction also find that, if they are experiencing continued relapse or deep, seemingly unresolvable feelings of hopelessness long into their sobriety, they are more than likely dealing with issues of untreated codependence. Many nurses report that their recoveries are supported with short-term courses of antidepressant medication in conjunction with nonmedical recovery activities.

Balance
The fourth category evaluated by our self-assessment tool was issues of moderation. This is commonly referred to as "operating in the extreme." Some believe this to be *the behavioral symptom* of codepen-

dence. As before, however, we believe these five issues cannot be separated if we are to understand the entire picture of codependence. We therefore evaluated nurses on this issue and included the data with the other four core issues.

This issue originates when a child observes and experiences the extreme behavior or thinking of his/ her caregivers. We easily can understand how this can be the case if there is an alcoholic in the home. It is less well-appreciated, however, that extreme behavior can also be something as seemingly innocuous as work addiction, where a parent effectively is "gone." Many children in these situations suffer a fear of abandonment, an emotion that "covers" the sense of shame they feel for not having the emotional nurturing they need. The shame belongs to the parent, not the child. The child merely acts it out.

The parent may be preoccupied with fear of financial failure or emotional inadequacy, or have little time to give to the child. In any instance of extreme "either-or" thinking or behavior, a child learns that wide extremes of behavior and feelings are "normal." When confronted with the crisis orientation of Western health care settings, he or she fits right in and perceives the environment as normal, which could not be further from the truth.

Only 78 percent of the nurses polled responded to the items addressing issues of moderation, indicating that they may not experience these issues in the ways the tool suggested. We note, however, of those who did respond:

- 59 percent indicated they experience these issues in their lives.
- 38 percent, or a little over one-third, perceive

themselves as feeling childlike in their responses to clinical situations.

- 21 percent, or about one-fifth, perceive themselves as supermature and superresponsible.
- 9 percent have issues in both extremes, and one percent feel they are appropriately mature for their age.

Issues of moderation effectively prevent a nurse from developing and maintaining a dynamic theory of practice and from living and practicing in a balanced way. The manifestation of moderation issues can sometimes be amusing, but the price we pay in terms of longing for inner peace and completion is very dear. Intimate relationships are seldom possible for people struggling with moderation issues.

For example: As a nurse, you may seldom make a mistake, but when you do, you experience shame or guilt as a result and don't talk about it. You are always able to get all of your work done, no matter how busy; *or* you can never seem to prioritize and get your work done, no matter how light the load. You are either told you can do the work of four people, *or* your colleagues experience you as unstable and unsafe, and abandon you by overtly or covertly telling others they don't want to work with you.

You may believe you are crazy and doubt the soundness of your clinical thinking, *or* use shaming rather than teaching while implementing your highly rigid plans of care, due to the resentment you feel when patients choose not to "do it your way." You may find yourself acting like a 5-year-old in intense clinical situations *or*, in the other extreme, acting like you have the philosophical calm and wisdom of a woman or man twice your age.

Perfection and control

The fifth core issue is the issue of realities. A functional family gives children the message that they are perfectly *imperfect*. This family teaches the child that perfection is not an attainable goal, and, as a result of their humanity, they will make "mistakes." We occasionally offend others with our feelings, our behavior, the way we look, the way we think—a functional family provides a child with the language to talk about this.

When we know and accept that we are capable of error and that we are not god or goddess of another, we become willing to be held accountable for those parts of our reality that offend or hurt or about which we feel shame. The key word is *shame*. Our own shame functions to remind us of our humanity. Whether female or male, the experience of shame feels the same. Common synonyms for shame are "embarrassment," "ashamed," "chagrin," "guilt," "humiliation."

From our shame, we can appreciate our imperfection, move through the feeling states that it invites us to embrace, and acknowledge the truth that we are not our own Higher Power. In turn, we are led closer to a sense of true humility, closer to a sense of a Power greater than ourselves, greater than our parents, greater than our colleagues, which ultimately gets us closer to love. Feeling our own shame, then, enhances our capacity to give and receive love.

If children are taught that a parent is god or goddess of the house and that they should "act like perfect ladies" or "perfect little gentlemen," or should be "seen and not heard"; or if a child adopts the mask of perfection and control in any part of his/her reality, then *that child's love is replaced by fear.* Robin

Norwood has written that children do this "to control every outcome so as to prevent chaos from happening" in their lives.[7]

Nursing environments encourage perfection. Get all your charting done on time, make sure medications are passed on time, get patients to ancillary departments or to the operating room on time. The profession encourages each individual to act, work, and function like a well-oiled machine. Do it perfectly, do it now. Such phrases as, "How could you be so stupid?" "God, you'd think as long as you've been a nurse you'd be able to ... (fill in blank)," or "What'd they teach you in that nursing school anyway?" are but three of thousands of shame messages we either hear or tell ourselves about our practices. We learned how to do it as children, and our professional environment reinforces it!

The pain we experience about having to "do it perfectly," whatever "it" is, characterizes the illusion that we are in control. Whether we control another's perception of us, or we control patients into thinking that we have the right answer about their healing process, we become *controlling*. From this position, true healing is not possible. If we believe we are perfect or have the "right" answers about healing, we block the ability of the universe to work its magic. We also discount the healing practices of others and, from this position of perfection, maintain a professional arrogance that we are right. More importantly, since some of the care that we provide in our "right" way does promote healing, our perfectionistic practices are reinforced—which, paradoxically, drives the disease of codependence.

The opposing extreme of perfection and control is

chaos. We appear professionally as one who is not "doing it," whatever "it" is. Nurses in this extreme are seen as out of control, chronically late to work, chronically sick. They have no faith, no organization, no ability to prioritize their care-planning, and they cannot be a channel for healing energy. In either extreme, colleagues say of one another: "This person is hell to work with."

In chaos, many nurses leave the profession because they feel they don't fit and can't handle the pain of feeling chaotic. The reality of their leaving, however, if they are unaware of the issues of codependence that underlie their pain, is that they will repeat the same pattern in another job, relationship, or activity. Or, as is more frequently the case, they will remain in the profession, cared for by the professional enabling of other codependents who will want to fix their pain!

The spouse who decides to leave a relationship with a practicing alcoholic will enter another dysfunctional relationship unless she/he enters recovery. So, too, might nurses maintain the legacy of spiritual upheaval they experienced in the profession and the blame they placed on the profession for their problems, transferring their dysfunctionality to an addiction, an illness, or another workplace.

All but two nurses, or 136 of 138 studied, indicated they feel controlled, perfect, and controlling. From this position, accountability, a developing spirituality, and a capacity to be creatively present for the healing needs of another are effectively stifled.

Data Summary
Cursory generalizations from the data on the

nurses we studied include:

- 96 percent have self-esteem issues.
- 84 percent have boundary issues.
- 93 percent have issues with wants and/or needs.
- 68 percent experience moderation issues.
- 99 percent experience reality (spirituality) issues.

The composite nurse from this study practices as a nurse feeling "one down," wide open and too vulnerable, needless and antidependent, superimmature, and controlled and perfect. In our opinion, nurses' goals should be:

- To practice from a position of having a sense of one's own value; that is, to be "self-esteeming."
- To support the value of others.
- To be appropriately vulnerable; that is, to capably protect and respect your own reality while doing the same for another.
- To function interdependently, with a capacity to ask—without shame—for needs and wants to be met.
- To support others in doing the same.
- To live and practice moderately from a theory of practice that promotes accountability and, thus, spirituality.

A theory of practice that does not promote health in each of these five core issues helps perpetuate the disease of codependence and fuels the confusion that surrounds the practice of nursing in this country.

Table 3. Codependence and Nursing Self-Assessment Inventory

Place a check by each statement that applies to you.

A3	___	To feel valuable as a nurse, I must be "needed" by my patients.
A4	___	I can complete all my assigned tasks at work during the allotted time without feeling shame.
D3E2	___	I become resentful when patients do not comply with treatment plans that I suggest.
A2E2	___	I believe I can function as a nurse better than most of my nursing colleagues.
E2	___	I have higher expectations of my work performance than others say is realistic.
B2	___	When patients feel emotional pain, I find myself wanting to leave the room.
C3	___	I leave work and have a drink just to unwind.
A3B3	___	When colleagues are angry or aloof, I believe their behavior is about me.
B3	___	I experience fear within the two hours prior to going to work.
D4	___	I am able to ask for support or help with my work when I need it.
D3E2	___	When I ask for help from a colleague and don't receive it the way I expect it, I become silent and resentful.
C4	___	I eat balanced meals at appropriate times.
B3	___	I feel depressed when seeing patients in pain.
D3E2	___	I often do more than is expected of me and feel resentful when colleagues don't do the same for me.
A3	___	I believe I am valued as a nurse for being good.
B3	___	I feel embarrassed when a colleague makes a mistake.

B3	___ I focus my nursing care on protecting others at all costs.
B3	___ I take responsibility for my patients' feelings.
C2	___ I put my patients' and my colleagues' feelings before mine.
B3	___ I am very sensitive to how colleagues and patients feel, and I often feel the same.
A2E2	___ I have definite ideas about how care should be provided by others and tell them when they're doing it wrong.
A2B2E2	___ I offer therapeutic advice to others without being asked.
A3	___ I agree with others' clinical opinions even when I disapprove, just to prevent feeling rejected.
B3	___ I sometimes pull off to the side of the road after leaving work, to catch my breath.
C2D3	___ I leave work and feel angry or resentful toward my children/mate.
C3D3	___ I like to shop after work as a way to unwind.
A2	___ I believe all this stuff about codependence is bunk.
A2E2	___ I believe others have problems, but my life is in perfect order.
A2	___ Some of my nurse colleagues are absolute wrecks.
A3	___ I feel good about myself only when I am caring for others.
C2	___ I do not ask for assistance from colleagues.
B3	___ I put myself in dangerous clinical situations.
D3E3	___ I procrastinate with difficult or unfamiliar procedures.
A3	___ I feel shame in asking for help when I am already expected to know how to do something.
C2	___ I am not aware of my feelings in difficult clinical situations.
C2	___ I am more nurturant of the feelings of others than of my own.

A3	___ I am embarrassed when someone compliments me on the care I provide.
A3	___ I laugh off compliments or change the subject to something else when someone praises me.
A2	___ Adult patients who bring stuffed animals to the hospital are foolish, especially male patients.
E2	___ My colleagues often tell me I am difficult to work with.
A2E2	___ I feel frustrated and angry when my family or friends don't take care of their health the way I think they should.
A3B3	___ I feel hurt or ashamed when a colleague expresses opinions different from mine.
E3	___ I am frequently told in my performance evaluations that I am not working up to my potential.
A2E2	___ When I evaluate employees, I frequently tell them they are not working up to their potential.
B2	___ There are times when I am snappy with patients, especially if they are demanding of my time when I have other things to do.
A3B3	___ I feel shame when other departments make mistakes.
A3B3	___ I feel shame when someone criticizes the nursing profession or the organization for which I work, believing in part that it's about me.
E2	___ When the emergency department is very busy, I am perfectly in control and aware of everything that's going on with every patient.
A2B2D2	___ I attempt to convince others of how they should be providing care in clinical situations.
A3E2	___ I am harder on myself about my clinical judgments than anyone else.
A3C3	___ When I make a clinical error, I use sex or chemicals to ease my feelings about it.

A2C2D2E2	___ I can remember the details of each time colleagues have hurt my feelings and take the opportunity to tell them about it from time to time.
E3	___ I make frequent medication errors but don't tell anyone about it.
C2	___ I distance myself from my own feelings by focusing my attention on caring for others.
A3C3D3	___ My professional self is different from my life-away-from-work self.
A3	___ If folks found out what I was really like, they would not like me.
C3	___ I am not within 20 pounds of my ideal weight for height.
A4	___ I am a lovable person and truly believe it.
B3	___ I have a difficult time working around drunk patients.
C3	___ I come to work with a hangover.
C3	___ I take sick leave when I could have told them at work why I really couldn't be there.
B3	___ I share the intimate details of my life with abandon.
B2	___ I trust no one.
A2E2	___ I am frequently let down by the behavior of others.
A3B3C3D3E3	___ I have been physically abused by a physician and decided it wasn't appropriate to report.
B3	___ I often allow people to hug or touch me, even when I don't want them to.
B2	___ I touch all my patients, whether I have their permission or not, because touch is very therapeutic.
C3	___ I frequently eat sugar during the shift just to have enough energy to keep going.
A3B3C3D3E3	___ I live with someone whose drinking or drug use concerns me, and I don't say anything about it.
A2B2C2D2E2	___ People have told me they are concerned about my alcohol or drug use, but it's not a problem for me.

54

A2E2	___ I believe codependence is a disease of weak-willed people.
A4B4C4D4E4	___ I have happy and rewarding intimate relationships.
A3B2	___ I frequently leave intimate relationships before the other person leaves me.
C2E2	___ My work life is serious business, as is my home life.
E2	___ I am always complimented on how neat my house looks.
A2B2C2D2E2	___ I am often told that I can do the work of two or more people.
A2B2C2D2E2	___ I am called supermom or superdad or supernurse (circle).
B2E2	___ I am always in control of my feelings at work and never show my true feelings in front of patients.
A3E2	___ I never wear the same uniform two days in a row.
A2B2C2D2E2	___ I can make better clinical decisions than most physicians.
A4B4C4D4E4	___ I believe I am enough.
A2A3B2E2	___ I call home frequently while I am at work to assure that everything's okay.
A3E2	___ I rehearse my conversations with colleagues before speaking with them so my words come out right.
A3B3	___ I worry about how others will respond to my clinical decisions.
A3B3E3	___ I feel embarrassed when colleagues tell off-color jokes but don't tell them about it.
A2C2E2	___ I am told that I occasionally offend people with my words, but it's not really true. They're just being picky.
A3C3	___ I find myself daydreaming a lot when I should be concentrating on something else.
A2E2	___ I tend to overcommit myself.
A3C3	___ Most of the time I feel different from the rest of the world.
A3C3	___ I frequently think I'm crazy.
A3B3C3	___ I have difficulty with physical or sexual intimacy.

A2B2	___ I use my intellect as a way of staying ahead of the rest of the nursing profession.
C3D3	___ I sometimes have explosive feeling attacks and don't understand why.
C3	___ Most of the time, I don't get what I want at work.
E4	___ I have been told by colleagues that I look inappropriate, but I have too much going on in my life to worry about that.
A3B3C3D3E3	___ I have been in several relationships where I have been physically, sexually, or emotionally abused but tolerated it because I believed it would get better.
A3B3	___ When someone is whispering, I feel shame.
C3D3E3	___ My work is mostly disorganized and messy, and colleagues tell me about it, but they're out to get me.
A2B2C2D2E2	___ I don't often take breaks because there's simply too much going on.
D3E3	___ My colleagues frequently pick up my workload for me.
B3	___ I have difficulty concentrating at work because there's so much going on in my life.
B3C3	___ I get scared when certain people touch me but I don't say anything about it.
B2C2E2	___ I never disclose my own feelings to patients as they are disclosing theirs to me because it is therapeutically inappropriate.
D3	___ I will express my feelings by whining or complaining to others.
B3	___ I trust everyone because everyone is basically good.
B3E3	___ I trust people who frequently let me down.
A2D2E2	___ I am always early for my shift, feeling angry or ashamed when others are late.
A2B2C2E2	___ When a colleague asks, "What's the matter?" I frequently say

	"Nothing," even when I feel emotional pain.
B2	___ I feel lonely much of the time.
A2E2	___ I talk about physicians/other colleagues to others, but rarely to their faces.
A2E2	___ I don't believe alternative healing practices have a place in contemporary nursing, especially with our advanced technology.
A3B3C3D3E3	___ I wear professional attire tight because it feels good, and I want to feel attractive to others.
C3	___ I will work overtime, feel guilty about it, and not charge for it.
B3	___ I do a good enough job and feel victimized by others who are critical of my work.
A4B4C4D4E4	___ I believe I am an excellent nurse and feel I function appropriately without fear, shame, pain, or resentment for my work.
C2	___ I rarely ask for help and feel resentful when others don't anticipate my needs.
A4B4E4	___ I am able to protect my thinking and feelings when confronted about them.
A2D2E2	___ If a colleague makes a mistake, I will tell someone else before I talk with him or her about it.
B3D3 E2	___ I feel resentful when colleagues take work time to have fun, especially when there's so much work to do.
A3B3C3E3	___ I feel shame when I overhear colleagues talking about patients in demeaning ways, but ordinarily I say nothing about it.
D3	___ I live on the edge most of the time.

Codependence and Nursing Self-Assessment Inventory Worksheet

Refer back to the Self-Assessment Inventory and place a check mark below, on the line corresponding to the letter-number combination indicated before each statement. Place a check on the line each time the letter-number combination appears. When you are through, the check marks will give you a fair assessment of where the bulk of your codependence issues exist and, consequently, some clues on where to begin your recovery work.

PRESUMED ENTRY-LEVEL QUALITIES	PROFESSIONAL CODEPENDENCE		DYNAMIC THEORY OF PRACTICE
Aware of Own Value and Capable of Supporting the Value of Others	A2_____ Arrogance Grandiosity Superiority	A3_____ Low Self-Esteem Professional Shame Issues	A4_____ Self-Esteeming
Appropriately Protective of Own Reality and Respectful of the Reality of Others	B2_____ Rigid/Walled Invulnerable Inflexible Unempathetic	B3_____ Too Vulnerable Carries Others' Realities	B4_____ Functional Boundaries
Appropriate With Needs and Wants and Capable of Encouraging Others to do the Same	C2_____ Needless Antidependent Inappropriate With Needs and Wants	C3_____ Too Needy Too Dependent	C4_____ Interdependent
Mature Within Age Level	D2_____ Supermature Moderation Issues	D3_____ Superimmature Moderation Issues	D4_____ Lives and Practices Moderately
Aware of Own Spirituality and the Evolving Spirituality of Others	E2_____ Controlled Perfect Controlling	E3_____ Chaotic Procrastinative	E4_____ Accountable Spiritual

Chapter IV Reference Notes

[1]Portions of the "Codependence and Nursing Self-Assessment Inventory" modified from *What is Co-Dependency?* (Phoenix: Co-Dependents Anonymous, 1988), pp. 1-3.

[2]Pia Mellody, *Facing Co-Dependence* (San Francisco: Harper & Row, 1989), pp. 7-42.

[3]Jael Greenleaf, "Co-Alcoholic/Para-Alcoholic: Who's Who and What's The Difference?" in Wegscheider-Cruse, et al, *Co-Dependency: An Emerging Issue* (Pompano Beach, Florida: Health Communications, Inc., 1984), pp. 5-17.

[4]Ken Wilbur, *No Boundary* (Boulder: New Science Library, 1989), pp. 45-59.

[5]Mellody, op. cit., p. 69.

[6]Ken and Mary Richardson, Barbara and Curly Munroe, *Loving the Child Within* (Phoenix: American Audio & Tape Library, 1988), tape series.

[7]Robin Norwood, *Women Who Love Too Much* (Los Angeles: Jeremy P. Tarcher, 1985), p. 211.

*This is one of those cases
in which the imagination
is baffled by the truth.*
—**Winston Churchill**

V

FACTS HIDE THE TRUTH

We believe that *facts can hide the truth*. We would like to approach this discussion from three perspectives. First, facts are useful and necessary components of our clinical practice. They are commonly our rationale for making clinical decisions. In many respects, our clinical thinking, guided by research and linear cause-and-effect thinking, promotes useful conclusions.

Our second perspective is that when nurses rely *solely* on factual, linear, research-guided models of care, they fail to integrate intuitive principles that have been known for centuries and that complete the healing process. These intuitive principles are feelings, ways of knowing answers to problems that either are not provable or defy scientific law. When applied to Western healing practices, alternative healing methods—certain forms of touch, energy balancing, psychic skills—often make no sense. Yet they work.

Not long ago, the physician to the Dalai Lama sat at the bedside of a dying patient in a university medical center in San Francisco. Attending physi-

61

cians, medical students, and nursing students watched. After 30 minutes of silence, he gave his diagnosis—a rare blood disease—confirming what his Western colleagues had spent days and thousands of dollars trying to determine. Research is useful. It also can pull us off balance.

As the nursing profession evolved in the United States, it moved away from valuing such inspired practices of healing and into a mode of practice based on fear and shame. Ninety-eight percent of nurses are women. And women in this country typically have had to justify their existence in a variety of painful, shame-inducing ways. It is no different in the nursing profession.

As theoreticians in nursing (mostly women) have struggled with these issues, much of the ground nurses have gained has been in the form of "prove it to us with facts." As a result, women in nursing have fought tooth and nail to be respected as practitioners of healing and have developed a practice which—by conforming to Western modes of research—has become stultified, bureaucratized, abusive, and far from methods of healing that they once knew worked. When facts—and facts alone—rule over the nursing profession, they can hide the truth about nursing.

This brings us to our third point: Facts, with no grounding in the day-to-day reality of nursing practice, can easily become myths and misperceptions. In what follows, we compare public and organizational myths and misperceptions about nursing (the *"facts"*) with the professional reality of nursing as we see it (the *"truth"*).

What do you believe?

In relation to stress-related illness: The *"fact"* is, nurses know how to take care of themselves and should be healthy. The *truth* is, nurses suffer from low back pain, chronic colitis and other gastric disturbances, chronic urinary tract infections, migraine headaches, high blood pressure, hypo- and hyperglycemia, skin diseases, depression, and other stress-related disorders.

In relation to addiction: The *"fact"* is, nurses know about, understand, and treat the diseases of addiction and, therefore, should not have them. The *truth* is, 80+ percent of nurses may be codependent and often medicate the pain of their disease with alcohol, drugs, food, sex, spending, gambling, serial unhappy relationships, and more. Nurses are just as addicted, if not more so, than the general population.

In relation to burnout: The *"fact"* is, nurses live to care for others and should love the rewards they get from their work. The *truth* is, a nurse's work often is demeaning, depressing, grueling, discounting, and demanding—and nurses do burn out.

In relation to parenting: The *"fact"* is, because nurses are natural caregivers trained to work with others, they should have excellent parenting skills. The *truth* is, nurses often bring fatigue, anger, shame, fear, pain, and job and financial worry into their home environments and have little energy for effective parenting.

In relation to spirituality: The *"fact"* is, nurses should be spiritually inspired healers. The *truth* is, nurses are required to accept physicians, other nurse colleagues, and institutions as gods, and they come to believe that they, too, can be in control. Spiritual practices and the art of healing are effectively shut down from this perspective. Ninety-nine percent of our study group, as you may recall, believe they are controlled and perfect on the job. Many nurses enter the profession with the altruistic ideal that they are called to the work in a deep spiritual sense. Many others, however, enter nursing because Mom or Dad choose it, it is a guaranteed job, they are single mothers wanting the safety of a guaranteed income, they sublimate their desire to go to medical school by becoming a nurse—anything but the notion that they are drawn to the profession through spiritual inspiration.

In relation to intimacy: The *"fact"* is, nurses really should know and understand people and have the necessary skills for intimacy. The *truth* is, nurses are invited to wear the mask of superhood and are discouraged in showing others who they really are. Nurses have a high rate of divorce and broken relationships, and they struggle with intimacy as deeply as anyone else who wears masks in relationships. Nurses often are too tired, too demanding, too frustrated, too walled-off, or too needless to experience intimacy at deep levels.

In relation to healing: The *"fact"* is, nurses are physical and emotional healers of themselves and others. The *truth* is, nurses have too little time for the healing of anyone due to personal and organizational demands and the fallout from the stressors of their work.

In relation to job performance: The *"fact"* is, nurses should be evaluated only on the quality of care they provide. The *truth* is, nurses more frequently are evaluated on everything *but* quality of care. Nurses are evaluated on criteria established to determine whether they have clean shoes (one nurse told us clean *laces*), whether their charting is legible (despite the hieroglyphic double standard of their physician colleagues), whether or not they are "working up to their potential" (a shaming message that says "Do more"), or how they look (Are you in the dress code? Is your hair off your collar? Are your colors acceptable? White sandals are not acceptable). We have long believed that the color of your clothing or whether your shoes are clean have nothing to do with the quality of care you provide. They merely create the *perception* that you are "professional" and have the ability to do it someone else's way.

We believe that to be truly helpful to nurses, job performance evaluations must include the component of value. That is, does the evaluation process value you for who you are *and* for what you do? Does this environment induce value-invoking, value-supporting policies and procedures, or does it shame you into conformity? As we evaluate recovery processes, more will be said about this issue.

The problem with research

Talking about codependence with nurses from an intellectual perspective is both useful and potentially dangerous. Codependents can effectively shield their issues from view with their intellects. This especially is true of nurses in a profession that is guided so thoroughly by research-oriented practices and, as a result of professional codependence, promotes arrogance, using walls for boundaries, needlessness, superhood, perfectionism, and unhealthy myths. There is every opportunity to avoid looking at these issues and to discount the truth by holding up our accomplishments or the unrealistic expectations of the medical profession and lay public.

Earnie Larsen describes the struggle of recovery from chemical addiction as the "struggle of the stuff of heroism."[1] Confronting a chemical addiction is profoundly heroic. We believe addressing ourselves to the issues of personal and professional codependence is *equally* heroic! We are not talking about easy stuff here! We are talking about moving away from intellectual banter into the feeling reality of the disease of codependence. To do otherwise perpetuates the shaming process and prevents us, the women and men who "people" the profession of nursing, from being capable of receiving what we give: love, healing, hope—a sense of community with others and ourselves.

Chapter V Reference Note
[1]Earnie Larsen, *Stage II Recovery* (San Francisco: Harper & Row, 1985), p. 4.

The cause is hidden,
but the result is known.
—Ovid

VI

SHAME IS THE "I AM" FEELING

Shame, as a feeling, has a bad reputation. Many people believe that recovering from codependence means we must eliminate shame. Not so. "Healthy shame" can be truly helpful in our lives.

Healthy feelings of shame function to let us know we are not perfect, we make mistakes, and we are no more or no less valuable than anyone else. From this place of feeling our own shame (which translates to embarrassment, chagrin, mortification),we develop a sense of genuine humility. From a place of humility, we recognize we are not gods—and our words match our behavior, indicating we truly believe it. We move closer to a sense of and appreciation for a Power in our lives greater than the limits of human understanding. Once realized, this sense of a "Higher Power" (the term developed in Alcoholics Anonymous to describe the existence of a power each of us defines for ourselves) leads us closer to love. Feeling our own shame, therefore, functions to bring us closer to love—closer to those qualities we had when we entered life: the capacity to give and receive love, the capacity for trust, truth, and intimacy.

On the other hand, feelings of shame can work destructively in our lives, particularly if we suffer from a distorted sense of our own value. It is presumed we enter nursing practice with a well-developed sense of our own value and the capacity to support the value of others—our patients, our colleagues, our families, ourselves. If we suffer from codependence, however, we often will have low self-esteem and a sense that we are less valuable than others. Instead of feeling "healthy" shame that helps us develop true humility, we feel *overwhelming* shame.

This overwhelming shame encourages us to tell ourselves such things as: "I am stupid," "I am ugly," "I am fat," "I am a liability," "I am too sensitive." This distorted, negative "I am" thinking causes us to feel badly about ourselves and then to choose behavior (e.g., "wearing masks") that hides or distorts these very painful feelings.

Nurses have been and continue to be the subject of studies that explore their low or nonexistent self-esteem. In many nursing settings, programs have been developed that attempt to address esteem issues for nurses (stress-reduction, assertiveness training, quality circles, etc.), most frequently to no avail. The mechanisms for working with issues of distortion in our sense of value are better understood today. Operating under the presumption that you entered the nursing profession with a well-developed sense of your own value and were capable of supporting and accepting the same in others, you would know that your professional behavior is less a reflection of who you *are* and more about what you *do*.

For example: You are a student nurse, training in a baccalaureate program in a large city. You are

68

currently studying medical/surgical nursing and are in clinical laboratory at a medical center. Your patient load consists of three patients: one just back from the recovery room who had surgery under a general anesthetic; an elderly man six days postoperative from a bladder operation; and a young man recovering from an appendectomy.

You are adjusting the IV on the postoperative patient, an elderly female with a history of congestive heart failure, and note the flow rate to be twice what it should be. The patient is semilucid from her general anesthetic and has just received 800 ml of additional fluid. You auscultate her lungs. You hear rales in both lung fields, her diastolic blood pressure is elevated, and her respiratory rate is fast, shallow, and labored. The charge nurse enters the room and asks your impression of what you see. You relate the findings, and she says to you, "God, what are they teaching you at that nursing school anyway? Honestly, baccalaureate students wouldn't know how to regulate an IV if their lives depended on it! Don't you know you can fluid-overload a patient with congestive heart failure?" She leaves the room. You stand there flooded with feeling.

Your shame, the feeling of embarrassment you felt when held accountable, even if abusively, would allow you to say something like, "I wasn't paying careful enough attention to the flow rate, and I'll try to in the future," or "I was in with the man in 214 thinking I had checked the IV on Mrs. Smith more carefully than I apparently did. What suggestions do you have for her care right now?"

If you have an operative "core of shame," however, your tendency would have been to spiral into a

69

pool of despair or worthlessness, feeling not only your own shame but the shame you brought with you into your adult relationships and nursing practice from your history.

Shaming messages

You may have heard the terms "shame core" (Mellody), "toxic shame" (Bradshaw), or "shame-based" (numerous authors, including Gary Trudeau in Doonesbury).[1] What these terms address is the pool of induced reality that a child accumulates as the result of childhood experience. This induced reality, as noted earlier, enters children (who have not yet developed functional boundaries) in three ways.

First, verbal and nonverbal *shaming messages* from primary caregivers or important persons in children's lives, direct children to begin defining their sense of value—who they think they *are*—based on the definition of others. If a child hears such statements as, "You are so clumsy," "How can you be so stupid?" "Grow up," "You have so much potential," "I should have had an abortion instead of having you," "All you do is take, take, take; you never give," and so on, the child translates these messages to "I *am*. . . clumsy, stupid, immature, not enough, a liability."

Shaming messages seem so innocuous. They are common to every family. The point at which they become part of the child's self-definition and, hence, sense of value, is when the caregiver fails to recognize that messages that shame the child must be rectified if the child is to grow up with a healthy self-image. Shaming children into conformity is a much easier way of getting them to "behave" than taking the extra few minutes to be creative in our parenting.

Shameful/shameless behavior

The second way a child takes on the "feeling reality" of others is through the *shameful behavior of others*. Caregivers (parents, grandparents, other relatives, siblings, or family friends) whom the child naturally loves, act irresponsibly with any part of the caregivers' realities—that is, they behave in ways for which they should feel shame. If they don't feel that shame, they then become *"shameless."* The adult behavior and the shame, plus the other feeling states associated with it, literally are shot into the child.

Since children have no means of discriminating that adults or "significant others" are acting irresponsibly—that their behavior is more about the caregivers and their histories than the children—the children absorb the shame belonging to the shameless adults. It becomes a part of who they believe they are, taking the form of an "I am" statement (usually "I am crazy," "I am hysterical," "I am out of control") and adding to the growing pool of messages they tell themselves about who they are.

For example: Our son Jesse is playing a video game on TV and has just accumulated 65,000 points ... his highest score. At this moment there is nothing more important to Jesse than his video game and the score he has achieved. Candace has to go to the market and, since Jesse is too young to stay home alone, Candace says to him, "Jesse, I'm sorry to have to interrupt you, but I have to ask you to turn off the TV now because we have to go to the store." Jesse's reaction is one you have all either heard or said yourself when you were a child. "But Mom, I have 65,000 points and I can't leave now!"

Candace has a choice. She can say something like, "I can't wait all day, Jesse, turn off the TV and come now." In his best whine, Jesse implores, "But Mom, I've never gotten this much before!" Candace has another choice. "Turn off the TV; we have more important things to do than play stupid video games all the time."

In the above example, Candace has shamed Jesse. She has acted shamelessly and sent him shaming messages; she has told him his wants are not important; she has implied she is the goddess of his life and can say or do anything to him whenever she wants; and she has given him the message that he is stupid for wanting to finish his game. Jesse takes on her shame, her anger, and her agitation. He retreats in silence, cries, or has a tantrum.

In a nonshaming scenario, Candace could have said, "Jesse, I know 65,000 points is a lot, and I wouldn't ask you to turn off the TV if I didn't feel leaving for the store was important right now, but it is, so I'm asking you to come." "But Mom, I've never gotten this much before." "I know, honey. You must feel really good that you've gotten such a high score. Chances are, if you've done it once, you can do it again. I know how important it is to you, and if we could wait, we would."

In the second example, Candace has not shamed Jesse. Instead, she has validated his score, has not discounted his value as a person, and has still made the decision to go to the market, since to leave him at home alone at his age is inappropriate.

Carried Feelings

The third mechanism that operates to create a

72

shame core is what Pia Mellody[2] calls *carried feelings*. You probably have had the experience of walking into a room and knowing someone is angry. You may not see anyone acting out, but you know that anger is in the room. Anyone who does not recognize and admit to any part of their thinking, feeling, or behavior—in other words their "reality"—sends that reality into their environment.

Children soak up the feelings of others like a sponge. They know when Daddy is angry or when someone in the house—like a depressed parent, for example—is in pain. They can tell without anyone saying a word. Similarly, nurses can walk into a room and feel other people's emotions. The nature of nursing work invites us to be hypervigilant. Our psychic antennae and lowered internal boundaries seem to require us to feel every feeling everywhere.

Caregivers, acting irresponsibly with their own realities, encourage children (whose ability to discriminate about the origins of the behavior and feelings of others is underdeveloped) to take on the feelings of the adults and act them out.

For example: Candace returns home at the end of the day with Jesse and Patrick—the three of them troop into the house with multiple bags, jackets, toys—and they discover David, sitting at the table, frowning. The air is thick with David's feelings.

Candace immediately gets busy, putting things away, starting dinner. After the obligatory "hi" has been exchanged, Jesse goes straight to Candace and says, "What's wrong with Dave?" Candace, after spending her life "in the middle," responds these days with, "You need to ask David, honey." Jesse approaches David and asks sincerely, "Dave, what's wrong?" David, if irresponsible, will respond with that one word we all know is untrue: "Nothing!"

What follows is a picture of an entire family acting out David's feelings. Patrick takes on David's withdrawal by checking out from everyone, crawling up onto his bunk, and playing with baseball cards. Jesse starts pushing on Candace, asking for things he knows he can't have or can't do, escalating in anger with each "no." He has taken on, and is acting out, the anger David feels. Candace has picked up David's resentment. Her carefree return home has developed into a silent diatribe. "Great! We can *never* come home in a good mood without David ruining it. And *I* did all the shopping and now *I'm* cooking dinner. I'm sure *I'll* be doing the dishes, too. And I do *not* want to hear about whatever it is he's making a big deal about today."

How could this picture have been changed? David simply says, "I'm feeling angry and resentful right now and I just want to sit here withdrawn for awhile." The difference in the outcome is amazing. Jesse and Patrick say, "Sorry, Dave." "Sorry, Dad." "What happened?" one of them invariably asks. If David feels it's appropriate to discuss, he might talk about it some. If he feels it's information not appropriate for children, he will say something like, "It's really adult stuff; you guys don't need to worry about it. I'll be back on track in a little bit."

Candace fixes a cup of tea and sits with David, asking, "Do you want to talk?" If David says he doesn't, Candace tells him she loves him and goes on with her plans. The boys play—free from the burden

74

of David's feelings. David has been responsible with his feeling reality. He has claimed it, named it, and thereby protected the rest of his family from his feelings.

The key message in this section is this: Shaming messages, shameless behavior, and carried feelings are the three primary mechanisms by which children absorb the feeling and thinking realities of others, leading to states of emotional overwhelm. For the child, it is this induced reality that becomes the shame core driving the disease of codependence. For the nurse with an operative shame core, it is this pool of carried feelings that perpetuates the disease in the practice setting.

Do you experience a shame core?

Whether we call it a shame core, pool of carried feelings, pit of toxic shame, or some other name, there are two ways to determine whether you have one. For the sake of consistency, we will use the term "shame core" during the remainder of this discussion. Determining whether you have a shame core will boldly affirm whether you are codependent. You may feel tempted to defend yourself against this information as you read, so we encourage you to be attentive and receptive. Your healing, your relationships, your work in nursing—perhaps your life—depend on making these connections.

It may be useful to remind you of our definition of codependence. We said, codependence is a disease induced by child abuse, that leads to self-defeating relationships with the self and others. The key here is "induced by child abuse." Recall that we said child abuse is anything that shames the child.

Shame attacks

The first way to identify whether you have an operative shame core is through the experience of *shame attacks*.[3] Shame attacks are clues that what we are feeling at the moment is related more directly to our pool of induced feelings than to whatever is happening at the moment. In other words, you've "hooked your history" and are acting from that place. "Hooking your history" is a symbolic dip into your shame core. When something occurs in the present about which we have feelings, codependents drop a probe into their core of shame that checks to see if any more of those feelings are stored there. If so, the additional feelings are pulled up and added to the present feelings about the moment. We wind up overwhelmed by feelings.

We react to our thoughts biochemically. We feel feelings in our bodies as a result of biochemical signals. In the experience of a shame attack, it is as if the thoughts that generate present-moment feelings are accompanied by a chemical messenger that dips into our center where the shame core is felt—where shaming messages, shameless behavior, and carried feelings of others live. The chemical messenger says, "Hi, got any shame in there? How about fear, anger, or pain? Any of that floating around?" It's the shame train... boxcars of historical baggage... miles of dead-end track. Shame attacks feel awful!

Recall the function of your shame. It reminds you that you are fallible and make mistakes and indicates behavior about which you are willing to be held accountable. A shame attack quickly leads you beyond this potentially healthy reaction to the feeling that you are *worthless*. When you feel worthless, you spiral into despair and plug in the messages on the shame tape you have in your head: "I am worthless," "I am stupid," "I am yucky," "I am a slut," "I am dirty," "I am clumsy," "I am a liability," "I am less than you." Whatever the "I am" feeling, it is anything but, "I am fallible and am going to make mistakes."

Commonly reported feelings and thoughts associated with shame attacks include: feeling nauseated, flushed, suddenly rageful, and unable to speak; wanting to race out of the room and never come back; wanting to divorce or leave your mate and never speak to him/her again; wanting to leave work in the middle of the shift and not return; ringing in your ears or sudden headache.

We frequently have had the experience of lecturing to a large group of nurses when one of them reports a sudden headache or feeling of nausea. If you have this experience while reading this book, read on, paying attention to what we're talking about at the time. More than likely the discussion points to an important clue in your history regarding the origin of the sensations.

Feelings in overwhelm

The second way to determine whether you have an operative shame core is to note whether you *"go on overwhelm"* as the result of what are supposed to be normal, manageable feelings. That is, when expressing anger, do you rage instead? When feeling fear, is that fear manageable, or do you tend to panic, become paranoid, or have phobias? With emotional pain, is that pain functioning to assist your growth as it should, or do you spiral into feelings of helplessness? When you are held accountable for your thoughts,

77

feelings, looks, or behavior, do you spiral into feeling you are worth less than others or into despair because of shame?

The change in feelings often is immediate, continuous, and something you feel powerless to control or stop. Often your reaction seems out of proportion to you and to others. It is important to note that shame attacks and feelings "in overwhelm" are thoroughly masked by one condition: rage. If you rage as a result of feeling shame, fear, or pain in overwhelm, you know that rage can effectively *cover* the state of shame. For some of us, shame, pain, and fear are so uncomfortable that we will pull up rage to cover these feelings. If you rage, begin paying attention to the feeling state that immediately preceded the rage attack. Chances are, the feeling will have been shame.

Shame binds

Gerschen Kaufman[4] has written pioneering work on shame. We will not repeat his work here. It is useful to note, however, that shame can be bound to anything. We draw your attention to this phenomenon to guide your inquiry and further study. You may feel shame for feeling shame; you may feel shame for feeling fear, anger, or pain. You may feel shame for having feelings of sadness, grief, loss, panic, rage, or physical or mental illness. You may feel shame for being male or female. The list is long.

The key to knowing whether you have an active, operating shame core is not so much that you recognize what other feeling states or behaviors are bound to shame, but rather that you *experience shame attacks or feelings in overwhelm*. If this is the case, you can know that you are experiencing feelings or engaging in behaviors that were induced into you and reinforced early in life, and you can begin a recovery process (Chapters VII-XII) that will reduce the size and impact of the induced states. Getting into recovery can lead you to more satisfying and functional personal and professional relationships.

Professional shame issues

How many of you have had the experience of working in nursing and experiencing a shame attack or feelings in overwhelm? If so, their origin is rooted more in your history than in any present situation.

A nurse colleague recently recounted this experience of a shame attack. Don was sitting at the nurses' station, asking a pharmacist, who was delivering medication to his unit, a question about a patient he was caring for. The pharmacist replied, "Look, I'm too busy to be answering questions. Besides, you should be able to figure out the answer." Don felt flushed and could not speak, and he recalls feeling about 8 years old. He walked away and sedated his shame by staying busy and silent for the rest of the shift. Don described his innermost feelings during the remainder of the shift as feelings of worthlessness, that he was a liability, and that he was stupid.

Tracing his history, Don remembered times in his elementary school years when his dad would be sitting in his chair, reading the evening paper. Don would approach his father with a question about his homework. His father's usual reply was, "I don't have time right now. Can't you see I'm reading the paper? I thought we had raised a more considerate little boy."

Don's recovery work around this isolated shame attack is to work to dispute the shameless behavior of his father. Intentionally or not, Dad had shamed him consistently. He carried Dad's shame into the workplace and found himself frequently confronted by it. Our tendency as clinicians (in the face of carried shame) is to blame it on the pharmacist, tell another colleague he's a jerk, or have a colleague who witnessed the event make excuses to us for the pharmacist's behavior, thus undermining trust and reshaming us in the process.

Other examples of professional shame attacks are these: You see a nurse being reprimanded by another nurse or patient, and you feel the shame of the experience *for* her. You might make excuses for her, try to rescue her, try to defuse the shame with humor. You might ask a question to interrupt or refocus the conversation on something else. Later, because the shame induced by the experience is so uncomfortable, you do what you can to sedate the pain. You might overeat. You might act out sexually through seductive behavior with colleagues or with people after work. You might self-medicate with alcohol or drugs. You might stay an hour after the shift is over, wearing the mask of superhood, not charging for the overtime.

In nursing, the likelihood of putting on a mask in the face of someone else's shameless behavior or shaming messages is greater than at home, since it is less acceptable to rage or to withdraw to our bedroom, a book, or a television set. Instead, we may care for others, get busy, become arrogant and "better than"; we may say nothing and boil over into an ulcer; we may clean the dirty utility room or find a new way to arrange the furniture on the unit. You may observe a physician being rough with a patient during a pelvic examination, only to make excuses to the patient following the procedure, saying things like, "He's such a good surgeon." You feel guilt *and* shame for not acting in advocacy for the patient.

We feel the impact of the shame core professionally as the result of the experiences we carry into the workplace, but our tendency in dealing with shaming messages, shameless behavior, and carried feelings in the workplace is to pin the reason on something or someone else—the administration, physicians, old nurses, young nurses, male nurses, less competent nurses, other people in other departments, other agencies. We may feel shame for the organization for which we work as a result of its reputation in the community. We may feel shame and anger appropriately directed at an organization that abuses its employees but lack the courage to address the issues in management meetings. When we do address the issues, we may be labeled as troublemakers, crazy, or unstable—or treated in ways that tell us our perceptions are skewed, leading to discouragement and self-doubt.

Dysfunctional families operate with three basic rules. The system is closed, the messages come from the top down, and there are secrets. Dysfunctional health care organizations operate much the same way. The secrets they keep often are masked by "looking good," allowing only certain issues to be discussed, and keeping nurses and their concerns for organizational issues diverted to the next crisis—instead of talking straight, listening, and dealing with issues as though nurses' perceptions mattered.

On the other hand, we've had many nurses tell us how little they trust the organizations for which they work, even though we know the organizations are functioning healthfully. The system is open, there are no secrets, telling the truth in the language of accountability is invited, feelings are allowed, mistakes are addressed appropriately and forgiven. Often, however, even if this level of health exists within an organization, nurses continue to criticize the management, administration, physicians, or other nurse colleagues as the result of their own codependence issues. Oddly, and understandably, they believe they are right. As a result of codependence, we have done more damage to one another than we realize. In Bradshaw's sense, shame at the professional level is truly toxic and can bring an organization and the nursing profession to a standstill.

The *hope* message is this: Nurses' contributions to the health of organizations have been numerous over the years. There are many reasons why this is so. Nurses often are more willing to look at their own behavior than other health care workers, and they invite their colleagues to do the same. Nurses have contributed visionary ideas to the development of healing practices in this country and around the world. Though the nursing profession is predominantly female, the men and women attracted to the profession are drawn to it out of a deep sense of spiritual connectedness that transcends their genders.

Nursing practice in this country, as it has been known for the past century, is in a period of profound transformation, guided, we believe, by those women and men willing to take a hard look at themselves and their relationships. The impact of examining and dealing with issues of codependence in professional practice places, while ultimately healing, initially is destabilizing and will have definite far-reaching effects on other health care workers in other professions.

Nurses for many years have served as models for change. Changes required in recovery from codependence, however, are initially painful for us and painful for others. The pain is truly the pain of *healing* rather than the pain of rewounding. When nurses begin focusing on themselves as individuals within a profession that is so other-directed, so perfection- and control-oriented, and so requiring of personal sacrifice; the impact on patient care will be profound.

The beauty of recovery from codependence is that this process invites solutions to problems that have been plaguing health care delivery in this country for years. Understanding shame is a crucial ingredient in personal and professional reempowerment. Sidestepping shame and its influences falsely empowers us with the illusion of control and, paradoxically, reempowers the disease of codependence.

Chapter VI Reference Notes
    [1]Gary Trudeau, "Doonesbury," *Universal Press Syndicate*, 1989.

    [2]Pia Mellody, *Facing Co-Dependence* (San Francisco: Harper & Row, 1989), pp. 98-99.

    [3]Ibid., p. 98.

    [4]Gershen Kaufman, *Shame: The Power of Caring,* Rev. ed. (Cambridge: Schenkmen Publishing Company, 1985).

Psychotics think two plus two equals five;
codependents know two plus two equals four,
but they can't stand it.
                                    —Anonymous

VII

THE PAIN OF REMEMBERING

We have reached the point in discussing codependence, in both individual and global perspectives, where readers may become uncomfortable. Questions arise: "Are they saying *I* have to get involved in this?" "Are they saying *I* have to 'go into recovery'?" "Are they saying *I* have to do something about nursing?" "Do they really believe I *can* do something about nursing?"

Resistance begins: "I just wanted information so I could handle Dr. Williams better." "I looked into codependence so that I could understand the attitudes of nurses under my supervision; I wanted some tools to deal with *them* more effectively." "I didn't seek out this information only to be told I have a problem and I have to recover."

At this point, we inevitably ask, "How do I know if recovery is something I need to pursue?" Our response begins with a definition of addiction used by Dr. David Smith, medical director of the Haight-Ashbury Free Medical Clinic: Addiction is "compulsion, loss of control, and continued use despite harmful consequences."[1] Interestingly enough, this entire definition can apply directly to codependence; however, we emphasize the words "despite harmful consequences" as the gauge to the need for recovery work.

If your personal life, professional life, relationships, parenting, and inner sense of "being enough" all are intact and working, you may not be dealing with the issues of codependence. If, on the other hand, things really aren't that great—you are in a marriage that isn't intimate, you can't seem to maintain a long-term relationship, your relationship with your children is difficult, you are in conflict with your supervisor or colleagues—you are experiencing harmful consequences in your life.

If you begin to have stomach pain or a headache an hour or two before going to work; if you feel you *have* to take something, drink something, eat something to relax after shift; if you're functioning at a high level at work but spend your time at home alone and depressed; you are experiencing harmful consequences. It isn't our intent to tell anyone they *should* be in recovery, or they *need* to be in recovery. Rather, we extend to you an invitation to examine how your life is feeling. We want to let you know there are ways to do more than survive, avoid, or endure those things that aren't working for you.

The present is directly related to the past

The beginning of recovery is remembering— remembering *accurately* what was going on when you were a child; remembering who were there as your caretakers, what happened, how you felt *then* and how you feel *now*; remembering what your caretakers looked like and how it felt to you in your house as a child. Most of us don't embrace with enthusiam this

86

idea of "dredging up the past." It is hard work. We often hear, "What good will it do? Things happened, they are over and done, I've had to go on and live my life. Why dig into it now?" Recovery requires the work of remembering because *the present is directly related to the past.*

Those things that aren't working in our lives relate directly to things we experienced or were taught in our families-of-origin. Without remembering, it is impossible to dispute the early messages about our value and rules for life that haven't worked—values and rules we embrace and function from as adults that compromise integrity, truth, authenticity, intimacy, and inner peace. Without remembering, it looks to us as though the present is simply about the present, and if we could just change husbands, wives, jobs, organizations, supervisors, or clinical arenas, we wouldn't be having these problems. How many of you have tried just that? How many of you have been shocked to find the same problems appearing again in the new situation?

Without exception, every codependent we have come to know has tried to change the present without looking at the past, and they all have discovered that their problems continue. Codependents begin to doubt their judgment. They experience the underlying shame messages that tell them there is something fundamentally wrong with *them* that creates chaos out of every situation. They believe they will never be able to "do it right." In the turmoil of trying to be different, yet experiencing the same pain over and over again, lies the missing information: *The present is directly related to the past.* Once they integrate this concept and *become willing to do the work of remem-*

bering, they begin a process that frees them from the merry-go-round of failure, pain, frustration, despair, change, failure, pain ...

More about remembering

Tracy, a 36-year-old woman whose mother is a nurse, had been working for months on an individual basis trying to incorporate the concepts of codependence and recovery into her life. Everything she had read or heard about codependence fit for her. She had lived as a "people-pleaser" (individuals who can't say no, even when they want to, for fear of abandonment or rejection). For 16 years she had stayed in a marriage that was oppressive, emotionally abusive, and filled with conflict. She believed her thinking was faulty, and she felt stupid, although she was actually bright and extremely talented. She had become alcoholic, and it was clear to her that she began drinking to mask the pain of her codependence. During her work in recovery, she joined Alcoholics Anonymous. She has experienced continuous abstinence from alcohol to the present. Tracy ended the marriage and began trusting her thinking and appreciating her talents.

Codependence, however, continued to be a part of her life in significant ways. She found herself still choosing men who were emotionally unavailable and emotionally abusive to her. She continued to develop friendships in which there was little reciprocity—she nurtured her friends but did not receive nurturing in return. She continued to be a "giver" surrounded by "takers."

In working with Tracy, we continually directed her attention to her family-of-origin. She was resistant in this area, while extremely willing to look at the present. She often said, "When I was a child, I knew my thinking and my feelings and I believed in them. Also, I was not abused! My father was alcoholic, but that never really affected me. It wasn't until I married Art that I started experiencing codependence." We encouraged her to accept the premise that she wouldn't have chosen Art or stayed with him for 16 years if she was as free of abusive messages and rules as she believed she was when she met him. She would not have been attracted to someone dysfunctional unless she, too, had some dysfunctional beliefs about herself and her life. She resisted and continued to work on the present.

We knew through experience that eventually the concept that the present is directly related to the past would be illustrated for Tracy in a way she could not avoid recognizing. As educators for her, our job was to help her incorporate the concepts, and trust that, after she had exhausted other avenues to recovery, she would be able to accept that remembering was *necessary*.

Why would Tracy have to "exhaust other avenues to recovery" before getting serious about remembering—the element of therapy that would help her the most? In our experience, "Yes ... but ..." is the common phrase we hear. "Yes ... but ... it's really not important to place so much emphasis on remembering. What's done is done. I'm living in the now." Or, "Yes ... but ... you don't understand! It's about my kids (husband, job, mother-in-law, physical disability, employees, etc.)."

Until we exhaust all of our skewed thinking and see clearly that it doesn't work, we won't acknowledge the importance of remembering. We will function like a poorly operating film projector. The problem is *internal* (a defective motor), but we don't usually consider changing the motor. Instead we try a different film, or replace a bulb, plug, or part. But new films and parts still project distorted images because the internal mechanism has not been fixed.

The breakthrough for Tracy began with a simple realization: She had not graduated from high school, and her parents did not know why. She called us with this information, knowing she had discovered something profound but not quite sure where it fit.

We began to work with the abandonment children experience when caregivers don't pay attention to them. We talked about how truly unusual it is for parents to have a child fail to graduate without, at the very least, knowing why. Functional parents would have been participating in the child's education long before graduation. They would have been aware of problems, looked for solutions, provided support and encouragement. Early abandonment and neglect paralleled the abandonment Tracy experienced in all her relationships. Remembering this one event—not graduating from high school—was the first connection Tracy made between the present and her past.

From that day, connections to her history came at a rapid rate, and Tracy continues to discover them almost daily. Her recovery from codependence has accelerated tremendously, and she reaps the rewards of that today. She will no longer stay in relationships that are not reciprocal; she is not attracted to unavailable men; she is working on filling the "empty space within" with a sense of herself; she is attending college.

For Tracy, integration of the principle that the present is directly related to the past was the key that unlocked the gifts of recovery. As long as she resisted remembering, she could go only to the shallow levels of recovery. Today she works in the deepest part of her being, knowing that the first step is always going to be remembering.

Why was it so difficult for Tracy to begin to explore her family-of-origin for information? Codependents view their families from one of two extremes:

1) More than lovers, more than friends, more than even our own children, we want to believe our parents have been close to perfect; and, if we know they haven't, we don't want to blame them.

-or-

2) We *know* our parents abused us, but we do not want to expend any energy on understanding the abuse or forgiving them; and we don't want to return to the pain of the past.

Tracy knew there was alcoholism in her family-of-origin, so she knew her parents weren't perfect. What she did not want was to blame them for her life's problems. She was not aware of the nature or the extent of the abuse in her family-of-origin.

From either of the above extremes, we know remembering is going to be painful. This may not be a conscious awareness, but it is there. As a friend once said, "We will go through a hell of a lot of misery to avoid a little pain!" Remembering obviously ends our ability to detach the beginning of our lives from the present. Remembering does not require that we blame, turn against, or destroy relationships with our parents.

In remembering, we are challenged to accept this truth: "My parents did the best they could do to love me. They did not intend to hurt me. I was wanted, and they gave me what they believed were the functional things to give a child. *And* some things happened in my childhood that hurt me."

It is quite difficult for codependents to accept this, because we think in extremes—"either/or." We have to struggle to believe that loving intent *and* painful consequences can coexist. We simply don't want to embrace the issue of remembering because we are confronted immediately with this struggle and can see no resolution to it. The resolution lies in accepting that both seemingly opposing statements are true. Our parents loved us, did the best they could, *and* some things that happened to us hurt us.

Can you remember?
Remembering isn't as easy as we might think. In fact, remembering is the most difficult work of recovery. There are many defenses to memory that block our ability to remember *accurately*. We have worked with codependents unable to remember anything until age 16. More commonly we see the ability to remember most of childhood, with a block of time missing. It is not unusual to hear, "I can remember up to eight and after twelve, but ages eight to twelve are missing for me."

The first defense to remembering was covered thoroughly in the beginning of this chapter: the belief that the present is directly related to the present, not the past. In addition, there is difficulty in discerning between true memory and stories we were told of our childhood. It may be surprising to discover that our memory of what it was like does not coincide with the memories of our siblings, and our parents may have a third picture of that time. It is crucial to filter out the stories of our childhood so that we can work with our *own* memories. Going to members of our family-of-origin for data can be helpful; it also can be quite confusing. It is not a guaranteed method of retrieving accurate information.

If this sounds like a no-win proposition, you are beginning to recognize why remembering is so crucial to recovery and why we indicate it is perhaps the most difficult work of recovery. The hope lies in this message: Once we have moved through the block to connecting our past to our present, we have indicated our *intent* to remember. This statement of intent initiates the process of returning memory. We may be skeptical about this; intent cannot be enough to lead us out of the confusing maze that remembering appears to be. It has been our experience throughout our own recovery work and in working with others, that intent is an extremely powerful tool. Once engaged, intent works for us without fail.

The mechanics of forgetting

In psychiatric nursing, you learned several defense mechanisms—words that associate behavioral and psychological phenomena. We will discuss the six that seem most useful in describing the mechanism leading to lost history and skewed thinking in relation to codependence. The three processes used in childhood that lead to lost data for the child are: 1) Suppression, 2) Repression, and 3) Dissociation.

Suppression is the conscious forgetting of data. When children experience or observe something too painful, too distressing, or too frightening for their psyche to accept and integrate in a functional way, they decide to forget it. If, for example, you witnessed a parent physically abusing another family member, or experienced this yourself, you might have found the experience too overwhelming to keep in conscious memory. To survive emotionally, you moved it to your unconscious. There it remains, buried alive; very much a part of you, but lost to conscious memory.

Repression is the automatic forgetting of data. As with suppression, if you experienced something in childhood that was overwhelming emotionally, the memory is automatically moved from your conscious to your unconscious. Like suppression, memory of the abusive experience is buried alive. These experiences do not necessarily have to be about physical abuse. If you have been ridiculed, criticized, or "put down" in the presence of your friends, the experience easily could have been abusive enough for you to have used repression or suppression due to the overwhelming shame of the experience.

Consistent or repetitive abuse results in lost blocks of time in our memory rather than lost, isolated experiences. The data from these experiences returns with our *intent* to remember as we are able to handle it. Because we are gifted with these mechanisms to protect our emotional well-being, we can continue to count on their protection with regard to the return of memory. Only as we are emotionally prepared to cope with the information will it return to us.

Dissociation, the third mechanism of forgetting, is a process we reserve for childhood experiences in which we believe our emotional or physical survival is at stake. In these instances of profound abuse, we dissociate, or literally experience consciousness leaving the body. The discovery of what occurs for the child during a dissociative experience came with witnessing the return of the dissociative data. Dissociative data returns through spontaneous regression.

Spontaneous regression usually occurs when we are working in at least a level-one hypnotic state, in processes guided by a therapist. Spontaneous regression also occurs during the experience of massage, when feeling touch in an area of the body connected with a dissociative experience triggers the regression.

Therapists guiding clients through spontaneous regression discovered the out-of-body quality of dissociation through clients reporting they were witnessing the event: a) standing to the right of it; b) from the ceiling; or c) at the bottom of a dark hole.

Let's look at some examples to clarify this phenomenon.

Molly

Molly is a public health nurse practicing in a rural area near Nashville. She has a varied practice and has entered therapy because her husband has rage attacks. She reports that every time he rages, she feels stark terror, cannot speak, and finds it difficult to protect herself and the children. Molly says she cannot understand her inability to act protectively, especially since she is frequently around rage-filled behavior in her practice setting and manages it comfortably.

During a session with her therapist, Molly is asked to work with an image. She is asked to imagine all the members of her family in the kitchen of her home when she was 8 years old. Molly begins to see the image and reports she is standing to the right of the picture watching everything happen. Her therapist encourages her to stay with the image and reassures her that she will be safe as she watches. Molly feels herself getting very small; she reports she now feels like she is 8 years old. She is hiding under the kitchen table, and her father is slapping her mother repeatedly. This is the memory Molly believed, at that time, threatened her survival.

In her regression, she is at level "a," to the right of herself, where she can see, hear, smell, and taste but cannot physically feel the experience. She has moved to the least-defended place children go when they dissociate. Molly stays with the memory, letting herself finally feel the emotions from the experience that happened when she was 8. It has taken her 32 years to retrieve this data. It has taken 32 years to emotionally integrate the pain, fear, anger, and shame connected with this memory.

Daniel

Daniel, an emergency department supervisor, is having some body work done, trying to relieve a spasm in his shoulder that has bothered him for as long as he can remember. The spasm is not constant and is exacerbated by stress. Therapeutic massage has been the most effective treatment. Today, however, when the muscle is worked deeply, Daniel drops into deep weeping. He appears to be "gone"—lost in the experience—and the massage practitioner is aware that touch has triggered a regression for him.

Daniel's practitioner is aware that Daniel is in a hypnotic state and is having a regressive experience. He encourages Daniel to speak of what is happening. Daniel reports he is up on the ceiling watching his grandfather throw him to the floor and step on his shoulder with his boot, yelling at him, "Don't think you're so big I can't take care of you and your smart mouth! It will be a long time before you can get by with anything with me!" Daniel is 10 years old during this experience. The dissociative memory is the picture Daniel sees of himself with his grandfather. This experience threatened his survival on a physical as well as emotional level.

Daniel has moved to level "b" during the experience—a more defended place than Molly used. From the ceiling, he has distanced himself more from the emotional and physical violence. He cannot feel, he has the choice to look or turn away, he can still hear and smell.

The massage practitioner stays focused and attentive with Daniel throughout the regression, encouraging him to trust that he can withstand the impact of the memory. When Daniel emerges from the regression, the practitioner checks to ensure his client is feeling "in the room," is acting age appropriately, and feels he is on the massage table. Daniel is referred for follow-up to a psychotherapist whose work the practitioner trusts.

(We urge massage practitioners who use techniques that trigger regressive experiences to do so with caution. Without the education, or sometimes even the awareness that education is necessary, taking a client safely through regressive experiences can be dangerously destabilizing. This is not a criticism of massage techniques or massage practitioners. Rather, it is encouragement for all massage practitioners to be connected with skilled mental health professionals to whom a client can be referred should this situation arise.

(As with our work as educators, appropriate referral is part of being responsible and accountable to our clients, accepting our limits, and being willing to keep the safety of the client a primary focus. We are always concerned to hear of any health care practitioner untrained in psychotherapy working without the support of the licensed therapeutic community.)

Penny

Penny, a hospice nurse, is attending an intensive therapeutic workshop focusing on codependence issues. She became aware of codependence when a colleague suggested she look at the effects her work with dying patients was having on her health.

She has found the workshop to be a disturbing experience for her, filled with stories from others in the group that ignite memories of her childhood. She is feeling fragile and vulnerable as the third day of the intensive workshop begins. A member of the group is working with the therapist, recounting an experience of incest by her father while she was hospitalized at age 4. Increasingly frightened, Penny feels dizzy and a sensation of spinning as she listens.

The cotherapist turns her attention to Penny, recognizing she is in regression. She asks Penny what is happening. Penny wails, "I'm falling down a black hole! I can't see anything! Make it stop!" The therapist takes Penny's hands to help ground her, begins to talk her through the regression, and advises her that at the bottom of the hole she will see a picture. She wants Penny to tell her what she sees.

Penny, in a "little girl" voice, begins to describe being in the hospital with ear infections and being touched by a doctor in "the bad places." Penny has retrieved dissociative data involving molestation by a doctor when she was a child. She is at level "c," the black hole—the most defended of the dissociative positions—to protect herself during the experience. In the presence of therapists equipped to deal with the pain of molestation as well as regression, Penny was ready to have the data return and emotionally safe enough to reexperience it.

It is unlikely that codependents will have spontaneous regressions in any arena where they don't feel safe and protected. This is not the kind of experience we need to fear happening at the shopping mall or the movies. Because this data is so intensely protected, it will be revealed to us only when all conditions around us are conducive to safety and support.

As we were trained to think, so will we remember

We refer to codependence as an induced disease because so many facets of the disease have direct connections to what we were trained to do or believe. In our families-of-origin, we were trained in ways of thinking that affect our ability to remember accurately. We not only used these ways of seeing our environment when we were children, we continue to use them today in looking at our past or present. The mechanisms we are about to discuss are pervasive and interfere in direct ways with our abilities as adults to remember our histories accurately.

Minimization is the first of these methods of skewed thinking. You might recall from your psychiatric nursing experiences that minimization is making something less impactful or important than it actually is. As a child, you may have been telling a primary caregiver about something that hurt you. You might have been told, "Don't make such a big deal out of it. What are you going to do when you have real problems?" Or, as a child, perhaps you were describing how you saw Mom's tendency to breach the confidence of friends by saying, "Mom, Joanne asked you not to tell anyone that! Why were you telling Pam?" Mom might have responded with, "Oh, Pam won't tell anyone, and it's not a big deal anyway. I just told one person." Mom has modeled minimization for you: a way of thinking that makes what you think and do, as well as what others think and do, less important than it really is.

If you carry minimization into adulthood and practice it for many years, you become able to minimize anything—your spouse's drinking, abusive behavior, the incongruencies at work, a colleague's clinical mismanagement of patient care, the severity of a patient's pain, friends who are consistently late. Looking at your childhood, you also are able to minimize anything—your parents' neglect of you due to work or other commitments, the knowledge that you were supposed to be the opposite sex, being drawn up into the conflicts in your parents' relationship. Instead of seeing these situations as they really are, you apply the "Don't make such a big deal out of it" rule because you were trained to think in this way. With

100

minimization, we make light of the abusive nature of the experiences that have led us to think in harmful ways as adults. At the same time, we often *deny* that we are minimizing.

Denial is the second and more intense method of skewing our thinking. Denial is a term common to nursing and to many health-related fields. In addiction treatment, denial refers to an alcoholic/addict who can see that someone else has a problem with chemicals but is unable to see their own problem. Denial, as a way of thinking, doesn't occur only in the arena of addiction. We were trained in our childhood to apply it to many areas of life. Denial says, "I can see you have a problem or that this is abusive for you, but it doesn't apply to me."

Perhaps you frequently heard your mother say she would never live with a husband like Mr. Jones, who came home drunk from the bar every night—while *her* husband come home at 5:00 every night and drank a fifth of scotch. She was unable to see that she was living with the same dysfunction; she was "in denial."

Perhaps your parents provided no limits for you in your childhood, and, as a result, you frequently found yourself in dangerous circumstances (playing around construction sites, crawling through drain pipes, handling dangerous weapons without supervision), while they spoke of how neglectful the neighbors were because they didn't provide music lessons for their children. In denial, they were unable to see that neglect takes many forms, and what applied to the neighbors also applied to them.

101

If this thinking was modeled for you as a child, you are probably still using it today. As you look at your life in the present, are you saying "I could not put up with a husband who sits around in his undershirt and never contributes to the family," while at the same time you watch your husband work 18 hours a day and fail to contribute time to the family? As you remember your childhood, are you saying to yourself, "I know Nick was abused because his father used to really whack him with that belt" and, simultaneously, "It was different for me; at least all my father did was lock me in the closet. No one physically abused me"? Minimization and denial keep us from remembering our past in accurate form.

Delusion, the final method of skewed thinking, is, as Pat Mellody affirms, "believing something in spite of the facts."[2] Delusion takes us as far away from accurate perception as we can get. In childhood, if delusion was modeled for you, you might have heard your parents claiming they had a wonderful, happy marriage, while at the same time keeping you awake at night with their arguments.

The point here is that they *believed* the delusion, and you learned the incongruent message that happy relationships contain nightly arguments. This simple example illustrates active parental delusion that not only was emotionally abusive to you but also taught you to think about intimate relationships in ways that lead *away* from intimacy. If you were trained in delusion, you will be using it today; and if you are deluded, you will not know it. Delusional states permit codependents to remain in the most abusive relational situations while believing everything is wonderful.

You may have found hairbrushes or hairclips in your car or phone numbers on matchbooks, experienced your spouse not being where he/she said they were going to be, walked in on phone calls that suddenly hushed when you entered the room, found unexplained withdrawals from the automatic teller machine. You may even have been told by friends that your spouse has been "seen with someone else." If, in spite of all these facts, you continue to believe that your contract of monogamy is intact, you may be deluded.

In looking at your childhood, you may be able to report that your mother abandoned you and your siblings for days at a time; she always returned with a new man you had never met; she bought new clothes, perfumes, and jewelry for herself while you and your siblings had inadequate clothing. As you report this, you may still say to yourself and others, "My mom took care of us the best she could; there just wasn't enough money; she would have been with us if she could have been." This is delusion—a way of thinking you were trained to use as a child.

Minimization, denial, and delusion are ways of twisting our thinking and are employed in an effort to keep us out of pain. The underlying messages are:

- Life is too hard to take as it is.
- Being accountable and responsible won't allow you to do what you want when you want to do it.
- You must learn to lie to yourself about what is in front of you.

When you begin to strip away minimization, denial,

and delusion, painful memory returns. When you look at your past and your present head-on, you have to face some uncomfortable truths about it all.

You also have to accept responsibility for healing the pain buried alive in you. Acceptance of this responsibility *is* the recovery process. It is what you can do for yourself to heal your wounds; to stop using thinking processes that enable you to avoid reality; to quit paying the price of forgetting how you spent your life because you have so much fear of remembering. The pain of remembering—yes, remembering *is* painful—is validating and healing at the same time. Remembering is the hardest and most important work of recovery.

Chapter VII Reference Notes

[1]David Smith, "Cocaine-Alcohol Abuse: Epidemiological, Diagnostic and Treatment Considerations," *Journal of Psychoactive Drugs*, Vol. 18, (2), April-June 1986, p. 118.

[2]Pat Mellody, personal communication, May 1985.

We end up at the same place we started,
so why bother to begin?
—**Barry Stevens**

VIII

SPIRITUAL CYNICISM: DEEPEST OF THE INDUCED REALITIES

In addition to biochemical influences, we believe addiction is a disease born of overwhelming feeling and skewed thinking. When we try to live with these overwhelming sets of feelings and thoughts, compulsive abuse of whatever we choose will at first give us a quick, and often enjoyable, escape. As the escape becomes the prison of addiction, we experience a sense of hopelessness and cynicism. We have become convinced, through our own recoveries from multiple addictions and through work with hundreds of recovering nurses and other addicted people, that the messages "don't try" and "don't trust" underlie most addictions.

Introducing choice

The addicted person has an extremely difficult time comprehending and accepting the fact that he or she has *choices*. This lack of belief in choices, and the consequent lack of both hope and a sense of connection to anyone or anything except the "drug of choice," drives the addict to compulsive behavior.

In treating addictions, one central ingredient exists in all programs that are able to assist the addict in long-term abstinence. This ingredient is *spirituality*. By spirituality we do not mean religiosity or a connection to any singular faith or denomination. We are talking about the belief in a power larger than the limitations of life as we know it. When the addict leaves the hopelessness and cynicism behind, discontinues giving power to another human being or "drug," and chooses to connect with a belief in some entity greater than the mundane qualities of the human experience, the compulsion to use the "drug"—and the obsession that drives it—can be lifted. We define spirituality as this *belief*—whether it be in nature, the order of the universe, energy, God, or whatever it is for you.

The introduction of the concept of spirituality saved thousands of alcoholics in the program of Alcoholics Anonymous and *completed* a treatment package that the medical/psychiatric community had developed. Treatment professionals have learned over the years that treatment programs without the spirituality component often are frustratingly unsuccessful.

Characteristics of spirituality in relationships

The concept of spirituality is a key element in the ability to disengage from substances, behaviors, or relationships that affect us to the point of harmful consequences. Is spirituality as significant in supporting relationships that nurture us? Let's begin with a definition of a healthy relationship. At its most fundamental level, *a healthy relationship has the ingredients of trust, honesty, and intimacy.*

Trust says we will gift one another by making

our relationships safe places to be. Trust is nourished by the repetition of events that lead us to believe we are safe. Earnie Larsen captures the ingredients of trust very succinctly, saying that trust is the feeling of certainty that you will honor me for what I do, you will honor me for who I am, and you will be emotionally responsible *with* me, rather than *for* me.[1] More often in nursing, we assume we are responsible *for* others—a fact that hides the truth!

Honesty and trust are tied together intricately. Trust, and therefore love, will not tolerate willful dishonesty. Honesty says we not only will be aware of willful honesty, but we will not engage in dishonesty by omission. Honesty requires our willingness to talk about what we really feel and think. The lens of trust and emotional responsibility is focused by self-honesty. Self-honesty is the only gauge we have for knowing whether we are trustworthy.[2] In relationships, if we wear masks to hide who we really are, we are emotionally dishonest and not entirely trustworthy; the images we project become blurred for us, our colleagues, and our patients.

Intimacy speaks of trust, honesty, and acceptance. The magic of intimacy occurs when we are trustworthy and honest at the deepest levels and accept these gifts from another. As we become more trustworthy, we are trusted by another. As we are trusted, we are invited to become more vulnerable. As we become more vulnerable, those in a relationship with us see more of us and, thus, have more to love.[3] With the invitation to trust from a friend, lover, or family member who is trustworthy, more of our true selves are available to be loved. The level of intimacy perceived by each person grows as the level of vulnerability of each is invited, accepted, and loved. The entire relationship becomes reciprocal and *spiritual*. We live in acceptance of one another, are loved more, love others more, fear less, and are capable of talking from the heart.

A relationship without spirituality is a frightening place to be. Spirituality assures us we are not alone. Spirituality assures us we do not have to be in control of others —what they do, what they feel, what they think. Spirituality gives us the courage to trust, to be honest and therefore vulnerable, and to live in acceptance of ourselves and others.

Spiritual cynicism

Without faith in a power greater than ourselves— greater than our parents, our partners, our jobs, our patients—we have difficulty with relationships that operate on other than surface levels. We often are afraid to be honest with ourselves or to believe in the honesty of another's love. Further, without spirituality, we find it impossible to believe in something better for ourselves. The cynical messages—from society, our families, our colleagues, our friends— that tell us to settle for less than trust, honesty, and intimacy in relationships nourish the delusion that we *can't* have a relationship on a deep level.

The messages we hear about relationships—"trust no one" and "believe in nothing"—are quite similar to the internalized belief system of the addict. Clearly, some pervasive, deeply integrated, harmful belief is held in common by many. We call this belief ***spiritual cynicism***.

As noted in Chapter II, Maya Angelou has added

to the inception of this concept. In a lecture on evil, she said, "When a child is born, she knows nothing. If she is abused, she begins to believe in nothing and grows to know the hopelessness of cynicism."[4] *It is this "believing in nothing" that creates spiritual cynicism.*

On a metaphysical level, children may not enter life as "blank slates," but without conscious memory they certainly are wide open to be defined by their environment. We believe children enter life with the capacity to give and receive love, but the skills in the *expression* of love often are not modeled for them, are processed out of them, or both.

We believe the phenomenon of spiritual cynicism is a result of childhood abuse. It is more widely accepted today that children have been profoundly abused not only if they have experienced physical or sexual abuse, but also if they have experienced emotional battering/shaming or intellectual shaming—or if they have witnessed any of this abuse happening to others. These children have been harmed by those caregivers they naturally would trust with their physical, emotional, and spiritual well-being—those they naturally would trust as their teachers and models for the skills (emotional honesty, acceptance, and a capacity for the expression of inner truth) of intimate relationships.

"Don't try" / "Don't trust"

A child raised in a physically or sexually abusive environment fails to learn the skills of trust, truth, and the ability to talk from the heart. Further, a child who is overcontrolled (i.e., given the message that perfection is an attainable goal) or is raised by care-givers who emotionally are unavailable due to work, illness, addiction, or other causes, fails to learn the essential skills of loving. These children fail to learn how to talk straight, be vulnerable with appropriate people, risk the challenges of self-honesty, and feel certain that they will be kept safe in intimate rela-tionships with others. These children learn instead the messages of spiritual cynicism.

Out of spiritual cynicism, we are told *not to try* in relationships: "If I'm honest, I'll just get hurt," "I'll be abandoned," "I can't believe it is possible to just accept myself and others—no one does that." Spiritual cynicism tells us *not to trust* in relationships: "Don't wear your heart on your sleeve," "It's human nature to attack a vulnerable spot, so don't show anyone yours," "Never let anyone see they have hurt you."

Spiritual cynicism possibly is the most profound, deeply rooted, and hidden of the induced realities. Induced anger, fear, shame, and pain can be identi-fied easily once we understand this concept. They are identified through ways of expressing feelings, cer-tain behaviors, and ways of thinking. Spiritual cyni-cism, however, lurks beneath the surface of all other induced realities. The power of spiritual cynicism is in its tyranny over decisions we make about our personal relationships and our well-being. Our ina-bility to recognize the presence of spiritual cynicism emphasizes the subtle quality of its power. Spiritual cynicism is reinforced by hundreds of cliches and by the general acceptance of its messages. It is a ruth-less, terrifying taskmaster—shrouded in and fed by fear.

Consequence of spiritual cynicism

The consequence of spiritual cynicism is the *void*—that most fearful place where nothing exists to hold on to, to support us, to nurture us; where wishing, hoping, or dreaming cannot exist; where choices cannot be made because there is nothing to choose. Most children do not have spiritual cynicism. Our experience with very young children bears this out. If we tell them it is not possible to get what they want, they will think of another approach, another choice, another dream. They have not yet experienced the void—the dark, bottomless pit of nothingness. Unfortunately, society's messages, parental messages, and peers' messages about the lack of possibility and choice often win out eventually. And the child, so full of hope, loses his or her belief in anything.

Chapter VIII Reference Notes

[1]Earnie Larsen, *Love Is A Hunger* (Minneapolis: CompCare Publications, 1979), pp. 31-75.

[2]Ibid., pp. 31-75.

[3]Ibid., pp. 31-75.

[4]Maya Angelou, "That Which Lives After Us," in P. Woodruff and H. Wilmer (Eds.), *Facing Evil: Light at the Core of Darkness* (Peru, Illinois: Open Court Publishing Company, 1988), pp. 21-36.

The greatest danger,
that of losing one's own self,
may pass off quietly as if it were nothing:
every other loss,
that of an arm, a leg, five dollars,
is sure to be noticed.
—Soren Kierkegaard

IX

PERSONAL RECOVERY

Reclaiming who you are

To work on recovery from codependence, we have to reclaim (acknowledge, accept, and love) who we are. So long as we harbor spiritual cynicism, we won't have the hope that anything we do will help. Therefore, to begin our recovery, we must learn to *dispute spiritual cynicism* in all areas of our lives and relationships.

The elements of spirituality that have led to healing for thousands of people addicted to chemicals also work to heal those who suffer from codependence. With the spiritual connection as a part of our lives, we learn we can dare to try and dare to trust. We learn to embrace our spirituality, and with it, our hope. Whenever you find yourself thinking, "What's the use? I might as well accept ...," or "Why should I try? It will never change," remind yourself that someone taught you to live with such hopelessness. Remember that you don't have to embrace that attitude about life. Turn around and look in the direction of possibility—and in so doing, turn your back on spiritual cynicism.

We hear many reports of physicians verbally abusing nurses. The stories usually contain some spiritual cynicism as the nurse describes her powerlessness, the lack of support from her supervisors or colleagues. "Sure, it happens all the time. There's nothing we can do about it."

Recently, one nurse told us how she disputed her cynicism about a physician well-known for his verbal abuse of nurses. She simply said to him, "I feel really afraid when you talk to me like this. I'm asking you not to continue doing it." The physician, although surprised, was not offended and has not repeated his abuse of her. She directly disputed her internalized rule about this situation—a rule reinforced throughout the medical community: "Why should I try? This is one thing that will never change."

Another significant part of reclaiming ourselves is *remembering who we were in the beginning and what happened to us*. This remembering takes years; in fact, we're not sure it is ever complete. After the initial pain, it becomes a fascinating investigation as we discover characteristics and idiosyncrasies and look back into our childhood to discover where they began. While we believe much of who we are is biological, we also believe much of who we are was created in our family-of-origin.

A very close friend who has been working on recovery for years, shared with us her most recent revelation. In her childhood, her family often accused her of being crazy and threatened to institutionalize her in a state mental hospital. In addition, her family gave out subtle messages that religion or spirituality of any kind were not sophisticated or intellectual and, therefore, not desirable.

Until she discovered that her great-grandmother was institutionalized for religious fanaticism and died in a state mental hospital, she had no idea why her family had placed such emphasis on these seemingly unconnected issues. Once she learned of her history, she could understand that "crazy" was an accusation carried by her father from his family's shame, that being institutionalized was part of her father's family history and, therefore, something to which he would refer. Religion was to be feared because it made people crazy.

Confusing pieces of her childhood fell into place for her, and with the sense of relief that came with the information, she learned that what was going on wasn't really about her after all. Her shame message, "I am crazy," was about old family shame, still alive and well. *Remembering* cannot be overemphasized as a recovery tool!

Self-love—knowing the "Child Within"

The recovery tool with the most impact for us and for most codependents who have experienced it, is the *reconnection with the "Child Within."* Some believe this to be simply reclaiming those childlike qualities that have been lost, such as the ability to play. Certainly this is part of it. The reconnection to which we refer, however, goes much deeper.

Reconnecting with the Child Within is a therapeutic process in which we image ourselves as children. We see again what most of us have forgotten—the perfection, the energy, the mischief, the interest, the willingness to love and trust, the beauty of ourselves as children. Seeing this image makes self-love seem like a very real possibility. If this wonderful, beautiful child is part of us, it certainly is a part we can love. We recognize as well that we did not deserve what happened to us as children, that there was nothing wrong with us, and that the messages we received weren't accurate.

Once the connection has been made through imagery, we encourage a renewed commitment to the child. This commitment is carried out in tangible ways:

1) Spending time with the image of the child every day.
2) Beginning to dialogue with that image.
3) Beginning and continuing to consider what would be appropriate for a child when making decisions about who will be in our environment. (We remind ourselves that we live each day with a child as part of us, and we examine daily situations with this question: "Would I force a child to live like this, work around these behaviors, enter this environment?" If we answer "no" to these questions, we can be sure we are willingly taking ourselves to unsafe places—physically and/or emotionally— and this does not constitute self-love or self-care. Techniques are used to protect the symbolic Child Within that are quite similar to caring for a biological child— leaving the child with a nurturing person, for instance, while we engage, as adults, in adult activity. For example, we will often find a message like this on our an- swering machine: "I'm leaving little Carol with you when I go to court today.")
4) Setting limits regarding the behavior of others.

116

5) Determining what we are willing to do for ourselves to support the health and well-being of the Child Within.

We begin to reparent the child in us in a more functional way, recognizing that every time we abuse ourselves through behavior or through negative thinking about ourselves, we abuse that beautiful child. When we talk about functionally reparenting the Child Within, we are referring to an *achievement*: We have recognized the dysfunction in our childhood, have acknowledged that it produced harmful consequences, have become aware of the price we paid for being parented dysfunctionally, and have done a tremendous amount of work to get to the point where we can begin to reparent in a different way.

Our sense of humor and our sense of possibility live in the heart of the Child Within. This is why the metaphor of the Inner Child is so special. Reparenting this Child Within, though it may seem like talking to the casaba melons, is, in Tim Franklin's view, "like watching a magician pull a rabbit out of a hat. You know how she does it, and you still want to see her do it again!"[1] Working with the Child Within is that simple, that profound, that magical. As in the case of the Solomon Islanders whose yelling kills the spirit of the tree, codependence kills the spirit of the Child.

Figure 1, page 118, illustrates the connections between living from the perspective of the wounded child or the healthy child. The idea of using a tree was the gift of a student in a class we took together at the University of California, Santa Cruz. She used a tree to describe her growth in recovery, the branches representing her multiple addictions.

Figure 1:
DEVELOPMENTAL MODEL OF THE CHILD WITH

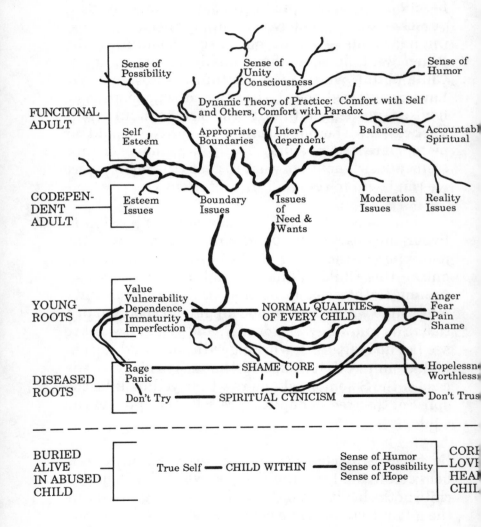

FUNCTIONAL ADULT

Sense of Possibility

Sense of Unity Consciousness

Sense of Humor

Dynamic Theory of Practice: Comfort with Self and Others, Comfort with Paradox

Self Esteem

Appropriate Boundaries

Inter-dependent

Balanced

Accountabl Spiritual

CODEPEN-DENT ADULT

Esteem Issues

Boundary Issues

Issues of Need & Wants

Moderation Issues

Reality Issues

YOUNG ROOTS

Value
Vulnerability
Dependence
Immaturity
Imperfection

NORMAL QUALITIES OF EVERY CHILD

Anger
Fear
Pain
Shame

DISEASED ROOTS

Rage
Panic

SHAME CORE

Hopelessn
Worthless

Don't Try

SPIRITUAL CYNICISM

Don't Trus

BURIED ALIVE IN ABUSED CHILD

True Self — CHILD WITHIN —

Sense of Humor
Sense of Possibility
Sense of Hope

CORI
LOVI
HEAI
CHIL

We have translated this metaphor into the five core issues of codependence. When a tree is planted in a healthy environment, all it requires for growth is sunlight, water, and the appropriate atmosphere. When a child is raised in a functional environment, he sends roots into a sense of his value, vulnerability, dependency, immaturity, and imperfection. If nurtured, the child sends deeper roots into healthy ways of expressing the normal feelings of anger, fear, pain, and shame. From this place, a child develops a sense of humor and creativity . . . from a core of love. The tap root extends deep into this core of love, creating a person who is comfortable with life's paradoxes and can laugh with them. From this core of love, the child is filled with perspective and possibility. Branches reach into the unknown, nourished by trust, truth, and faith.

When a tree is planted in an abusive environment (lack of water, stagnant atmosphere, inadequate nutrients, no light), it develops a more shallow root system. It may become brittle and fruitless, or may look healthy, but bear diseased fruit. A child raised in an abusive environment sends roots past the healthy places in his or her soil, beyond the capacity for appropriate expression of what lies below ground, and into a pool of overwhelming feelings fertilized by shame. Beneath the induced feeling states in which it grows lies the rich compost of spiritual cynicism that feeds the shame core. The child learns to wear masks, does not trust, has no faith. The branches such a child sends from the darkness into the light are stiff and barren and produce toxic fruit. It's better to learn to talk to the melons!

There are increasing numbers of therapists throughout the United States who recognize the value of working with the Child Within, and who either have developed a model or have been trained in a model for doing this work with their clients. We strongly recommend work with a therapist to rediscover and reconnect with your Child as one of your beginning steps to recovery. This may be the sweetest gift you ever give yourself.

Acceptance of self

With the determination to dispute spiritual cynicism, the intent to remember accurately, and reconnection with the Child Within, you are prepared to travel the path of recovery. The journey you undertake will lead you to acceptance and integration of all of who you are. But this journey will take work. For most codependents, acceptance and integration is difficult because they don't know who is "in there" to accept or integrate. Working on the "core issues" is one tool that will be a great help in finding out who is "in there" and in accepting that self.

Work on the core issues

Several writers emphasize focused work on *"core issues."* This is a highly useful metaphor since all of the symptomatology of codependence can be traced to one or more of these five categories.

Pia Mellody's work in codependence divides the disease into five core issues: Esteem, Boundaries, Wants and Needs, Moderation, and Reality. We recommend her book for a thorough examination of the core issues.[2] However, speaking briefly to the content of these issues and what they mean may be helpful in guiding you to deeper work on them.

Issues of esteem originate from having our value discounted, denied, ignored, or disputed during our childhood, leading to the development of a core of shame. The result is low self-esteem. Self-esteem is not an issue that originates primarily in adolescence as the young adult-child seeks affirmation of his or her value from peers. Children begin esteeming themselves from the inside out, or the outside in, as the result of messages received much earlier in life. Your work on issues of esteem is to reduce the size of the shame core by disputing the shaming messages you carry from your childhood.

Issues of boundaries originate from having your vulnerability as a child discounted, invaded, or unsupported. The results are dysfunctional or nonexistent boundaries. Having boundaries is not the same as "setting limits." Boundaries are beliefs about our physical and sexual rights and about our emotional and spiritual protection. Codependents will feel either too vulnerable or mask this vulnerability with invulnerability. Your work is to learn to contrive functional boundaries for yourself.

Issues of needs and wants originate from having our needs and wants as a child discounted, ignored, or neglected. The result is feeling too needy and too dependent on others. Some codependents mask this by acting needless and antidependent. Your work on this issue is to learn the difference between wants and needs as well as problem-solving strategies for meeting your needs and responding appropriately to your wants.

Issues of moderation originate in having extremes in thinking or behavior modeled for you as a child. The result is feeling superimmature in the world. The mask that covers your immaturity is supermature behavior. Your work on this issue is to seek moderation and learn to live in moderation—a condition initially quite uncomfortable for the right/wrong, either/or, black/white, good/bad thinking orientation of the codependent.

Issues of reality originate in having your physical appearance, how your body feels, your thinking, your feelings, and/or your behavior as a child discounted, ridiculed, or neglected. The result is internal chaos, often masked with perfectionism and control. Codependents may have difficulty acknowledging what they look like, how their body feels, what they think, what they are feeling, and what behaviors they use. In addition, they will be resistant to the concept of imperfection (the "good and perfect one") or live in the opposite extreme (the "bad and rebellious one").[3] Your work on reality issues is to examine each of the categories of reality (looks, behavior, thoughts, feelings) and learn to know who you are in these contexts.

This is a difficult journey—some call it the "hero's quest." It takes tremendous courage, tenacity, willingness, and faith. We have found it extremely helpful to reinforce our commitment to recovery with specific programs that keep us on track and give us information we need.

There are three sets of tools we recommend for recovery. Working on the core issues is the first of the tools we have found invaluable in our own recoveries. As we have witnessed the recoveries of others who are aware of the core issues and are working with them, we see that understanding the depth of their disease and what to do about it is greatly enhanced. Work on the core issues shows us a great deal about who we are—who we need to love and accept. To summarize the benefits of work with core issues:

- They focus attention on a manageable package of five key symptoms of codependence.
- They work.
- You feel better.

Twelve Step programs

Twelve Step programs are another extremely valuable way to learn about ourselves. Alcoholics Anonymous was the first Twelve Step program. Out of their success in helping those who suffer from the disease of alcoholism, the Steps have been applied to many painful human situations. The five Twelve Step programs that speak to the issues of codependence most thoroughly are: Al-Anon, Alateen, Adult Children Anonymous, Co-Dependents Anonymous, and Coda-Teen.

Many other Twelve Step programs have been formed to address specific recovery issues for specific groups. Attending meetings that are geared to specific professional categories (therapists only, physicians only, nurses only), while providing support unique to professionals' issues and allowing a freer climate of sharing, unfortunately also reinforces a sense of uniqueness. This attitude of "being different from others" leads to isolation from the rest of humanity—one of the fundamental issues addressed in recovery from codependence!

We challenge you to courageously share your recoveries in *generic* meetings. A codependent is a codependent, an alcoholic is an alcoholic, a sex addict is a sex addict—whether a physician or a fry cook, a therapist or a gardener, a nurse or an unemployed single mother of three children. We all face the same issues! Twelve Step program specialization beyond the generic issues deludes us into thinking that we cannot get what we need if our patients hear that we are sick too. Paradoxically, patients who are aware that we experience the same issues are more likely to ask for our assistance outside the context of meetings because they know we "walk the talk."

Many therapists and nurses argue that they cannot go to meetings without clients or patients "bothering" them for a little free advice about their health or a particular recovery issue with which they are struggling. If you experience this, do the work required to learn how to set your boundaries, ask for your need for privacy to be respected, and continue your work in therapy.

We support whatever choice of Twelve Step program you make, since the keys to successful use of the programs are learning to use the Steps, hearing the hope of others, and returning the gift of recovery to others through service to the fellowship. We also invite you to use rigorous self-honesty in examining your thinking if you believe you can't share your recovery with others who deserve to hear your experience, feel your strength, share your hope.

Through Twelve Step programs, you will receive support, guidance, and direction. You will discover who you have been and who you are. You also will discover your spirituality through consistent support for and acceptance of your willingness to love yourself.

A note about addictions

Recovery from codependence is not possible until a stable program of abstinence from chemical addiction is in place. We would be irresponsible to suggest you begin recovery from codependence while actively engaging a chemical addiction because:

- Chemicals sedate your feeling and thinking reality and distort the processes of remembering, while simultaneously feeding the shame.
- The issues of codependence are *powerful*. Examining codependence without a foundation of recovery from chemical addiction leads to relapse.

We do not believe, however, that a fixed period of abstinence (one year, two years) before addressing codependence can be generalized for those recovering from chemical addiction. Addiction treatment providers working simultaneously with mental illness and addictions, adolescents' issues and addictions, women's issues and addictions, and other multiple issue situations have proven this. For example, if an adolescent in treatment for a chemical addiction has suffered incest or been molested in his or her family-of-origin, failing to address the issues of sexual shame *in treatment*, with staff skilled in the management of these issues, is likely to lead to relapse.

If we fail to address the shame issues of women in treatment, or reshame them with attempts to treat their issues in the same ways we treat men's issues, they are likely to leave treatment and relapse. If we address women's issues of sexual shame in mixed group, we risk reshaming them. The converse applies to men with similar shame issues.

Contemporary treatment that fails to understand the nature and dynamics of induced realities, treating everyone with Twelve Step program processes only, misses an opportunity to stabilize adequately those who seek their assistance.

We believe each individual must be evaluated according to criteria that considers their readiness to explore codependence recovery. They must be guided by models that individualize their treatment plans and assess their readiness to examine issues of codependence in safe but timely ways.

Therapy

Another tool we have found valuable in recovery is *therapy*. We begin with a warning. Codependence has become one of the "hot topics" in psychotherapy. There are therapists who have added this specialty to their advertising without actually exploring codependence or consistently looking at their own issues of codependence. The disease attracts those of us who would esteem ourselves by caring for others and those of us who would avoid our own pain by taking on the pain of others. Therefore, a therapist providing clinical work in codependence recovery not only must be facile with the concepts of codependence but also understand the dynamics of shame, how to utilize Twelve Step processes, and how to assist you in effectively connecting your history to the present.

We advise you to screen therapists as you would any professional, asking specific questions about how they treat codependence, what techniques they use for family-of-origin work, what work they do with the Child Within. Further, do they understand the dynamics and strategies for working with induced shame, anger, fear, and pain? Do they understand the subtleties of childhood abuse and its relationships to adult codependence and addictive behavior? Do they understand the subtle power of spiritual cynicism, and do they support your work to dispute it?

You have the right to ask these questions and to expect truthful responses. If you sense the responses are not truthful, do not work with the therapist! Therapy with codependence initially is more directive than passive or reflective—meaning the therapist takes a more active role in your process. Therapists, like nurses, become frustrated with clients. They are human. The key to success is a therapist's willingness to be your guide rather than your guru. We personally have experienced therapy with a qualified therapist and have found it to be an excellent tool supporting self-revelation and self-acceptance.

In addition, there are specific therapeutic models designed to reduce the size of the shame core—vital, critical work in recovery. Your therapist can guide you through the process of uncovering your shame messages and disputing them, discovering carried feelings and returning them, and reparenting yourself with love and respect.

The journey of recovery from codependence cannot fairly be presented as simply reading a few books, attending a few workshops, or completing a 28-day treatment program. It is only fair to speak honestly of the qualities of recovery from the beginning. Initially, you may look and feel worse as you begin to work on getting better.

Initial recovery in codependence includes dropping defenses, feeling incredible emotional pain, and losing the ability to stuff feelings and to continue to operate in the world as we have before. The first year of recovery, in particular, is one when our "insides" (pain, fear, often depression) and our "outsides" begin to match. We haven't seen a client yet who didn't look and feel worse during the first year of recovery.

We have all worn our masks so long—for protection and to be accepted and loved. When we begin to remove the masks, taking a look at who we are, showing the world who we are, we need a great deal of support and all the tools at our disposal to handle the journey. Alone or without support, recovery is not worth the price of the trip! The first year of recovery is a year of grieving. The tools we discuss here help us move through this courageous process with goal-oriented direction and nurturing support. Qualified therapists assist us by providing tremendous depth to our recovery work.

Judy: one nurse's recovery

Judy is a veteran nurse with 28 years in the nursing profession. She came to counseling in chaos, wanting to leave nursing, wanting to die. In her first counseling session she said, "I feel like I'm just letting myself die, and I don't really care." She looked gray, old, and exhausted. She talked rapidly, alternating between humor (and cynicism) and despair. She recently had placed her 18-year-old son in treatment for alcoholism and had been told during the family program, "You are codependent and need to do something about that." .

Judy initially felt hopeless, defensive (she felt the label "codependent" referred to something about her that was undesirable and did not understand code-pendence was *her* disease), dishonest, unclean, "trashy" (her word), and victimized by alcoholism (her father, her ex-husband, a son, a daughter, and now her youngest child—all alcoholic).

Judy began the process of recovery with education about codependence—where it comes from, why she had it, how it manifested itself in her life and relationships. She was quick to grasp the concepts and moved rapidly into working with her Child Within (Judy Lynn was the name she was called as a child). Once reconnected to Judy Lynn, Judy felt overwhelmed by the sense of being dirty, trashy, and full of shame. Through the ensuing months she explored her childhood experiences.

Judy was raised by an alcoholic father whom she loved and whom she believed loved her, but who was frequently unavailable to her. He was either physically gone (and reappeared without consistency) or he was "gone" behind alcohol. Her mother was mentally ill. She had one younger brother. In her childhood, her parents cared for her brother but not for her. They gave him music lessons, encouraged him in school, and provided him with ample clothing, food, and hygiene products. Judy received none of these things. Her parents completely neglected her needs for emotional and physical nurturing.

In addition, Judy's brother ran the house, made the rules, and physically abused her. On one occasion, psychiatric aides took Judy away in a straight jacket after her mother called the hospital, blaming Judy for property destruction actually done by her mother during a raging episode. Judy frequently was shamed by her mother's bizarre behavior. Mom would appear in the neighborhood delusional, in various states of inappropriate dress, exhibiting explosive feeling states.

As Judy continued through the months of remembering, she embraced Judy Lynn, talking with her every day. She became aware, in a very real way, of how wounded Judy Lynn was as a child. She became very protective of Judy Lynn as she moved through her days. Judy was experiencing intense pain—she was grieving the loss of her childhood, the loss of functionally loving parents. She carried overwhelming shame as the result.

She began attending Co-Dependents Anonymous and became aware of her lack of boundaries as a result of listening to other codependents share their recoveries. She felt *their* pain and found it difficult to attend meetings because she was unable to protect herself from the pain of others. She began the work of creating functional boundaries for herself.

After several months of "working the program" of Co-Dependents Anonymous, working with Judy Lynn, working in counseling, and working on the core issues (introduced to her in counseling); Judy began the process of therapeutically reducing the shame core. Through therapeutic process, she gave back the carried feelings she had that didn't belong to her. She returned shame and the "dirty" and "trashy" feelings to her mother. She returned pain and shame to her father. She gave back all she had discovered she carried for others. Judy welcomed the work, saying that each time she did it, she felt great relief.

At her one-year anniversary of beginning recovery, Judy's family and friends could hardly recognize her. She was exercising, she had her eyes cosmetically reconstructed to remove the heavy lids that aged her appearance, she laughed frequently, she shared with a group of women quite openly, she was doing service work for Co-Dependents Anonymous—she had begun to feel excitement and joy again. Judy had detached from the enmeshment she had with her children and was living her own life for herself. She had integrated Judy Lynn, so that the child was no longer viewed as a separate entity, and began the process of functionally reparenting herself.

Judy's recovery progresses because she actively works her recovery program. She has terminated therapy for now but knows she will return if she needs support. When we saw her last week she told us, "The one thing I know now is that I want my life—every single day of my life—even the ones that hurt. I never knew it could be like this!" Judy's story is not unusual, but it is a testament to the courage required to begin this journey and to the transformational gifts that await us as we move along the path of recovery. Further, she remains in the nursing profession—more functional, better able to distinguish her own process from those of her colleagues and patients.

Becoming authentic

Prior to recovery, codependents often cannot accept praise, feel love from others, or live without fear. This is due, in large part, to our lack of authenticity. We know we are wearing masks, and we know we change them often—depending on who we are with, what is expected of us at any moment, and what arena we are in (being one person at home and a different person at work, for example). Because no one ever sees who we really are, when someone talks about us, we know they are talking about the mask we have shown them. They are saying the mask is pleasing to them and that they love the mask. On some level we are thinking, "Of course you do! I knew what mask you wanted, and I put it on! I knew you loved this mask, and I wanted you to say you loved me, so I'm wearing it! I wish I could feel like you love *me* instead of my mask. I keep wearing the mask to hear 'I love you,' and I keep feeling lonelier and lonelier."

The gift—the wondrous gift—of self-love and acceptance is authenticity. We discovered an unexpected blessing in doing the work of recovery: We discovered that showing ourselves to the world meant hearing the world talk to us about who we really are. We were no longer always pleasing to those around us, and that was frightening at first. In our authenticity, we no longer put on masks to control what others thought of us. Sometimes, people didn't like us, weren't interested in knowing us, disagreed with us. It was uncomfortable.

And when people talked to us about caring for us, about finding us funny or interesting—when people said "I love you"—the words came inside and touched our hearts. We knew they were talking about us, not a mask. We more frequently found ourselves filled with warmth as we felt the caring of others. We found ourselves feeling safe as we knew we didn't have to monitor our pretenses anymore, feeling deeply honest with ourselves and others in a way we had not understood prior to recovery. The value of authenticity is in knowing, many of us for the first time, that someone has seen who we really are and loves us just that way. Until we experienced it ourselves, we didn't know what we were missing!

132

Chapter IX Reference Notes

[1]Tim Franklin, personal friend and psychotherapist whose work with the Child Within is magical.

[2]Pia Mellody, *Facing Co-Dependence* (San Francisco: Harper & Row, 1989), pp. 7-42.

[3]Ibid., p. 113.

The times can be exciting
if we do not practice
the rigidity of our disease
by resisting new ideas and approaches.
—Anne Wilson Schaef

X

PROFESSIONAL RECOVERY: OVERCOMING BARRIERS

The current nursing shortage in the United States was discussed in a recent article by Dr. Margretta Styles, Livingston Professor of Nursing and former dean of the School of Nursing at the University of California, San Francisco. In her article, Dr. Styles noted two primary reasons for the nursing shortage: 1) statistical (as noted in Chapter II) and 2) hidden factors. Among the hidden factors noted were "physical and psychological overload."[1] Though perceived, perhaps, as causal, we believe the physical, emotional, and spiritual "overload" that nurses experience in their practices are direct results of the issues of codependence.

The American Nurses' Association, the National League for Nursing, and other national and state organizations are working to create strategies to address the nursing shortage. We believe such strategies must incorporate curricula and programs that directly address the issues of personal and professional codependence if they are to clarify the root causes of the shortages and the unhappiness that has plagued nursing practice for years. Creating sophisticated plans to address shortages, burnout, stress-

135

related illness, job performance, and management strategies will fall short unless we understand codependence and give *every licensed nurse* the opportunity to look squarely at whether codependence affects his or her life.

Why professional recovery is necessary

Professional recovery from codependence is necessary for three reasons. First, recovery is necessary from an *emotional* perspective. Nurses pay a tremendous emotional price for not recognizing and talking about the pain, fear, anger, and shame they carry into their private lives as a result of their professional experiences. Conversely, unresolved issues of codependence carried into the workplace are fed by the shame, fear, anger, and pain available in the professional environment for nurses to "fix." As a result of codependence, nurses suffer from depression, anxiety, suicide, addictive disease, and emotional, physical, and sexual battering—both on and off the job.

The second reason professional recovery is necessary is *physical*. Nurses experience physical disturbances resulting from the shaming process; their inability to say no to increased work demands due to understaffing; addiction to the alcohol, drugs, and sex they use to sedate the hopelessness and worthlessness they perceive in the workplace; and a variety of stress-related illnesses that take years off their lives.

Third, professional recovery is necessary for *spiritual* reasons. Nurses must be invited to practice from a foundation that acknowledges their unique, research-based contributions to the art of healing. Codependence encourages nurses to believe, however, that research-based practice guidelines and perfection-oriented thinking puts them in charge and *responsible* for the healing of others. This couldn't be further from the truth.

This attitude interferes directly with existing or developing spirituality. It says we can trust only *ourselves* to be sure all aspects of healing are covered—implying that we trust only that research-based part of ourselves. There is no room in this perception for developing the intuitive gifts we all possess. The loss of intuition in healing, we believe, is a loss of fully 50 percent of a nurse's tools. The loss of spirituality is not only a loss of connection with a Higher Power, but the loss of a "heart connection" with our colleagues, our patients, and our practice.

Barriers to professional recovery

At the head of this chapter is a quote from Anne Wilson Schaef. When she speaks of the "rigidity of our disease," she speaks of the behaviors and beliefs that prevent us, as professionals, from recognizing codependence and doing something about its influences. There are a number of significant influences that are important to address. They are summarized in Table 4 below.

Table 4. Barriers to Professional Recovery

Defenses	**Professional Abuse Issues**
Suppression	Physical Abuse
Repression	Sexual Abuse
Dissociation	Emotional Abuse
Minimization	Spiritual Abuse and
Denial	Spiritual Cynicism
Delusion	
Professionalization	

Defenses

Defenses that prevent us from seeing how codependence affects us personally also prevent us from seeing its effects professionally. *Suppression, repression,* and *dissociation* can create "lost history" in our professional lives. These mechanisms help us to forget painful experiences in the workplace by sweeping them under the rug. They enable us to move painful professional experiences out of conscious memory to the unconscious, where they can be retrieved only through a structured process of remembering. We feel their influences, however, as we project their disturbing features into the professional nursing environment with our words and actions.

Minimization helps us say "Things aren't all that bad" in the face of double shifts, understaffing, inadequate services for women, lack of services for the poor, abusive colleagues, compressed wages, and shortages of qualified nurses to function at all levels of care. It is true that many nurses throughout the United States are working to address these inequities. It also is true that if you learned to minimize in your family-of-origin, you most likely will minimize the magnitude of these issues, as well as the efforts of your colleagues and yourself to address the transforming changes that are occurring—and need to occur—within the profession.

Minimization, driven by the disease of codependence, has allowed the American Medical Association to create a proposal to bring Registered Care Technologists into the practice place. Registered Care Technologists would replace or support certain "technical" nursing functions. It is presumed by those who support such a role that RCTs would be an answer to the nursing shortage. From literature available through the American Nurses' Association,[2] this clearly is not an answer to the nursing shortage; but it is, once again, a way to minimize the importance and value of the role of nurses in health care. The proposal to dilute the nursing role with Registered Care Technologists is short-sighted and unsafe! Further, it is a means of reshaming nurses.

Some may view the preceeding as a political assault on the AMA or on physicians generally. It is not. It is, however, a challenge to the disease of codependence, which creates "quick fix" solutions to deeper problems. Adding RCTs as a solution to the nursing shortage is like changing the film when you need to change the projector.

Denial, another barrier to professional recovery, gives us such messages as, "I can see you have problems, but I don't," "I can see your facility has problems and is going down the drain, but ours is supported by NIH grants, so we'll stay afloat," and "I can see problems in nursing all over the place, but the medical profession doesn't have those kinds of problems." We may move from job to job, expecting things to be different, only to find them the same.

Delusion, a mechanism that causes us to believe things are factual despite the truth, says to us, "Just hang on a little longer. When RCTs enter the practice place, the heat will be off," or, "Yes, I was raised in an alcoholic family, but it didn't affect me. My life runs perfectly!" We use delusion to pass responsibility for our own skewed perceptions to our workplaces, physicians, insurance carriers, other nurse colleagues, and other organizations.

Marie, a hospice nurse, has worked with dying patients for seven years. Coming home from work one evening, she pulls into her driveway two hours late. John, her husband, leaves the garden to greet her. While hugging her, he says, "You know, honey, I missed you today. I feel like we're growing apart. I need more time with you."

Marie, tired and overwhelmed, says, "You think you're the only one around here! You should be grateful you're not dying of a terminal illness. I'm caring for people with problems a lot more serious than whether we spend time together. Besides, who's making the money here?"

Operating from a shame attack, Marie has minimized John's reality and discounted his needs by denying his feelings. Further, she is deluded about the impact of her work life on her primary relationship.

Professionalization, closely related to delusion, is another type of defense. It invites us to mask our dysfunctionality behind "looking good"—behind being "professional." We delude ourselves by looking good to the community, looking good to one another, and esteeming ourselves by "doing" to shore up the image of the profession. Professionalization creates the false sense that everything is wonderful in the health care delivery system.

Looking good in the context of the dysfunctional family is a role adopted by family heroes—those individuals who continue to strive for outside accomplishments to sedate the shame and pain of living with out-of-control behavior at home. Professionalization, the hero's role in nursing, invites nurses to gather "other-esteem" as a way of drawing attention away from the dysfunction within the profession or themselves.

At many levels, the nursing profession is a dysfunctional family. We interact with other professionals who are given the power to be "above us" or "give us orders." While simultaneously striving to maintain integrity with our professional identity, we deny certain feelings and perceptions, and keep certain secrets. Resentment, bitterness, frustration, disbelief, and a sense of hopelessness and helplessness result. From this well of confusion, we scapegoat one another, feel lost, or laugh it off. Our integrity as a functional family is lost in the fray.

Professional abuse issues

Recall our definition of professional codependence: "Any act or behavior that shames and does not support the value, vulnerability, interdependence, level of maturity, and accountability/spirituality of a nurse, patient, or colleague." Discussing professional codependence directs our attention to the shaming process within nursing. For ease in understanding, professional abuse issues are divided into four categories.

Physical abuse

Physical abuse in the workplace occurs overtly and covertly. Striking a nurse; throwing an instrument, chart, stethoscope, or other object at a nurse; or grabbing, shoving, or pushing a nurse all are examples of overt physical abuse. A nurse who witnesses a colleague being abused in this way is as severely abused as if she were the victim herself. In either case, someone is acting shamelessly. Nurses with inappropriate boundaries may accept or tolerate the inappropriate behavior.

Covert physical abuse of nurses occurs when we watch or receive reports of a patient being physically abused by a colleague, and we do nothing about it. Rough treatment during an intrusive procedure, such as a pelvic examination, that does not appropriately respect a patient's boundaries; touching a patient without invitation or without appropriate explanation, especially those whose level of consciousness is altered; the inappropriate use of restraints; and minimizing or denying a patient's or colleague's physical pain—all are physically abusive to you and to the patient.

A word about touch. Touch—making, restoring, or maintaining the physical bridge between you and a colleague or patient—can be therapeutic. When evaluating whether physical abuse is occurring in your professional environment, ask yourself how you feel inside as you watch others in the environment interact with their physical realities. If you feel at all uncomfortable as you do this—nauseated, afraid, angry, helpless, wanting to leave the room—chances are someone is using touch in shameless, inappropriate ways; and their shame is there for you to take on board. If you have an active shame core, this professional shame will be dumped right into it. These feelings do not occur when touch is given and received in a clean, therapeutic way.

Sexual abuse
Because the nursing profession interacts with

patients and colleagues in extremely vulnerable situations, and since we are all sexual beings, sexual abuse issues tend to go unnoticed unless they are overt. Overt sexual abuse is easily seen and reportable. Nurses are called upon frequently to intervene as advocates for sexually abused patients or clients.

Patrick Carnes has written the pioneering work regarding sexual addiction.[3] Schaef has extended Carnes's work to include issues not previously discussed or explored.[4] We refer you to both writers for a more thorough understanding of the dynamics of sexual addiction and "cosex" addiction. (Cosex addiction is a set of feelings and behaviors that keep us connected to another's inappropriate sexual behavior. We lose sight of our own sexuality and our belief that we have a right to protect and respect our sexual reality. We say "yes" when we mean "no." We manipulate and control others' beliefs about our sexual reality.)

According to Carnes, sexual addiction takes place at three fundamental levels. Level I includes compulsive masturbation, obsessive sexual fantasies and compulsions to act them out, sexual namecalling, shaming sexual gossip or joketelling, and prostitution. Level II includes voyeurism and exhibitionism (peeping and flashing). Level III includes such sexually violent crimes as rape, incest, and molestation. It is the Level III issues of which nurses are aware most frequently in the workplace, with children who have been victims of incest or molestation, and with women or men who have been sexually battered or raped.

The Level I and Level II issues are less obvious, less frequently reported, and less well-appreciated by nurses as impactful issues. But it is at Levels I and II where the majority of sexual abuse of nurses occurs. And the effects of this abuse are just as shaming and devastating as Level III effects.

Sexual jokes, sexual inferences, being called "honey" or "dear" or "sweet thing," are funny to some, shaming to others. In most contexts, they are sexually abusive. The operating room, critical care units, and emergency departments are especially visible places where sexual inferences are made through joketelling and slanderous gossip. This does not imply that sexual abuse does not occur in other nursing arenas.

A female nurse circulating in the operating room where male physicians are telling sexual jokes is being sexually abused—so too is the anesthetized patient! A woman undergoing postpartum episiotomy repair who overhears her physician ask her husband, "Want me to take an extra stitch for you?" is being sexually abused. A nurse overhearing the same conversation is as deeply shamed as the patient and her husband.

You may say things to yourself like, "Here he comes again, I don't want him touching me," avoiding conversation or contact with an offender. Once sexually offended by a colleague, you will be less likely to trust his or her professional judgment. Further, you may not have a safe place in the workplace to discuss these issues. You may feel nausea or panic, be unable to speak, have a shame attack, or pull up rage to protect your reality in the company of an offender. You may become silent or distant, saying nothing. These are a few of the many reactions reported in relation to sexually shaming experiences in the workplace. Because issues of sexuality and sexual expression have wide ranges of tolerance in this culture, nurses frequently are reshamed by those who fail to understand the impact of Level I and Level II behavior.

It is not as important to engage in a campaign to stamp out verbal sexual slurs as it is to assist ourselves and our patients in establishing and maintaining appropriate sexual boundaries. If you were sexually shamed as a child, the likelihood is considerable that you will not perceive this seemingly innocuous behavior as abusive. The degree of sexual shame you carry into your professional life from your history, how sexuality issues were addressed in your family, and what beliefs you hold as values in relation to sexuality will determine the nature and extent of your reaction to sexually shaming experiences in the workplace—and your willingness to respect the sexual reality of others.

Other issues of sexual abuse occur between colleagues concerning sexual preference and life-style choices. Homosexual men and women experience sexually shaming messages in the nursing profession in very abusive ways. We often have overheard conversations containing sexual judgments and sarcasm aimed directly at homosexual men or women. Many heterosexual men in nursing have been sexually shamed by colleagues or patients assuming they were homosexual simply for being male in a predominantly female profession. Many heterosexual women in nursing have been sexually shamed by their colleagues or by patients for "looking gay." Many homosexual men and women in nursing have been denied access to clinical or management positions because they had the courage to let their sexual preferences be known or because upper echelon management suspected they were homosexual. Such discrimination against our colleagues because of their sexuality or sexual preferences is sexually abusive, with its origins in the shaming process. It is rooted in the fear, arrogance, and pain of the disease of codependence.

Another type of sexual abuse involves colleagues who are seductive with their dress, behavior, language, or thinking. Wearing tight clothing, low-cut necklines, strong colognes or perfumes; exposing themselves to others while dressing in a locker room; inappropriately exposing patients during intimate procedures; snuggling up to a colleague with a sexual hug or allowing another to give a sexual hug—all are actions that inject sexual shame into the environment and into those witnessing the behavior.

Patients also can be victims of sexual abuse. Any professional behavior that supports shaming sexual myths or inappropriate sexual information given to a patient or client is sexually abusive. For example:

You are a pediatric nurse practitioner making rounds on several children in an acute care facility. You enter the room of a 9-year-old boy and find him masturbating. Rather than saying "excuse me" or something similar, you say, "It's not okay to be doing that stuff here," or "Keep that up and you'll go blind." In the latter examples, you have sexually shamed the child and given him inappropriate information about a normal sexual activity.

Other examples of sexual abuse include: minimizing a patient's sexual reality following the experience of an offensive sexual act, discussing sexual information or a heart attack patient's libidinal concerns within listening distance of other patients, discounting or making fun of a patient's sexual reality, providing inappropriate information regarding communicable diseases, and making judgments about a patient's sexual preferences.

Sexual abuse can occur easily in an arena that includes various states of undress, intrusive procedures, and altered states of consciousness as well as a frantic pace, crises, exhaustion, and frustration—to name a few of the variables involved. It is important for us all—physicians, nurses, others—to be aware of and know how to appropriately address sexually shaming experiences. Equally vital is our commitment to giving this subject the attention it deserves.

Because of the shame that sexual abuse generates, the degree of sexual abuse tolerated within an organization can break a nurse's ability to function from a centered, focused place. We have the right to say "This is offensive to me" and expect to be heard. We also have the right to nonshaming treatment while developing strategies that promote understanding and respectful action on the part of every health care provider in relation to the subtle power of sexual shame.

Our patients have the same rights. As their advocate, it may be your role to protect their sexual boundaries if they cannot do it for themselves. This is a tough challenge. One nurse, trying to reduce sexual abuse within an organization, risks a great deal. Many nurses, speaking the same language and supporting each other, become effective agents for change.

Emotional abuse

Nurses often believe they have to tolerate the emotionally abusive behavior of others in the clinical setting. It is one issue to learn and practice strategies in managing the emotionally abusive language or behavior of patients. It is another entirely to tolerate the emotionally abusive behavior and actions of our colleagues. Yelling, screaming, sarcasm, silent withdrawal, namecalling, racist or ethnic slurs, verbal attacks on a nurse's thinking or feeling processes, attacks on a nurse's professional actions, discounting or minimizing the relevance of a nurse's clinical judgment, gossip, slander, unrealistic expectations of a nurse's clinical performance, overcontrolling subordinates, lack of guidance with problem solving, and inappropriate intervention with a colleague suffering from addiction are all emotionally abusive.

Some examples of emotionally abusive actions toward patients are: shaming a patient into conformity ("If you don't learn how to self-administer insulin, you could die"), bringing a patient into conformity by lying for a colleague or stretching the truth (dishonesty by omission), bringing in colleagues or family with views similar to yours to "persuade" a patient to conform to a treatment objective, and telling patients to "just do it" rather than providing time, attention, and direction to help them understand a treatment plan.

Witnessing emotionally abusive situations can cause patients and medical personnel alike to carry away the feeling that they are "less than" others, feel the shame of the offended or the offender, act as if nothing had happened, stay sick or get sicker, or adopt a mask of needlessness and feel tremendously resentful. The behavior that emerges as a result of emotional abuse confuses even the most diligent nurse manager. Managers frequently see clinical behavior that does not match dialogue. They experience colleagues overtly complying with policies and procedures but still having behavior problems due to the pain of emotional abuse. Emotionally abusive colleagues often are labeled "passive-aggressive" and can be as frustrating to confront as a person with a borderline personality disorder. Emotionally abusive messages leave us feeling shamed, confused, and disillusioned.

Spiritual abuse and spiritual cynicism

Physical, sexual, or emotional abuse of a nurse by a colleague, manager, or supervisor; or a nurse inappropriately addressing or failing to address the physical, sexual, or emotional abuse of a colleague, patient, or family member, constitute *spiritual abuse*. This behavior says, "I am the god or goddess of this place and of your life, and I can do or say to you whatever I want, whenever I want, and there is nothing you can do about it."

We introduced spiritual cynicism in Chapter VIII. Spiritual cynicism tells us as nurses *not to try* to create healing changes within the profession: "Why bother? They're just after the bucks anyway"; "Give me a break; this place'll never change as long as doctors have control through money and power." Spiritual cynicism tells us as nurses *not to trust* our colleagues or one another: "She's just going to gossip about us anyway"; "He's on a power trip, and nothing's going to change him. Besides, if I tell him the truth, he'll just laugh it off"; "We might as well have Registered Care Technologists—nurses are nothing more than glorified technicians anyway."

Our most frustrating experiences in working with spiritual cynicism in the nursing profession come as we discover our *own* internalized messages of spiritual cynicism, to which we were initially blind. This is our challenge to every nurse who helps or seeks to help others in the practice setting: Do more than give a passing glance to the foundations of spirituality so needed in patients'—and your own—recovery processes. As James Bugental notes, "A person comes to psychotherapy out of a sense of possibility, a feeling that there is the potential for life to be different than it has been."[5] This sense of possibility is *hope*—alive, but buried beneath the messages of spiritual cynicism.

Without consistently confronting and questioning our own skewed thoughts and feelings, there is little integrity and much inauthenticity in our work with others. Patients know when our words don't match our behavior; so do our colleagues. When we say to them, "Have hope," "Try," and at the same time model our own hopelessness about our compulsive overeating, the organization in which we work, or our relationships, our patients and colleagues note the lack of congruence.

They are far more likely to let our behavior reinforce their cynicism than they are to adopt a new way of looking at their healing simply because we encourage them to do so with our words. Struggling with and embracing our own messages of spiritual cynicism, and sharing our struggle with our patients and/or colleagues under appropriate circumstances, creates the spiritual bridge that taps into their sense of possibility and gives them hope.

Nursing care that does not integrate spiritual principles or that medicates the pool of induced feelings, thoughts, or behaviors as they are expressed, misses a tremendous opportunity. Effective assistance with these issues requires more than revising management strategies. It requires each of us to be trained to think about and treat codependence and other obsessive/compulsive behaviors at deeper than surface levels.

Spiritual cynicism ultimately may reveal itself as the most profound consequence of abuse. It is one of our prayers that nurses increasingly hear the value in trying, in hoping, in trusting, in believing that love is more powerful than fear. It is our belief that dysfunction in the nursing profession could not survive in an environment of faith, and that with faith, nurses would experience the level of professional relationships they so deeply desire—and deserve. Spiritual cynicism is a message of distorted perception, fed by fear, that feeds the shame core, sustaining the disease of codependence. Change within the profession of nursing is not possible when the dynamics of spiritual cynicism operate in our professional relationships.

When nurses, counselors, therapists, physicians, and others understand the relationships between their own spiritual cynicism and a patient's ability to confront the same in themselves, our work to create change in our dysfunctional thought systems will carry a message of hope and possibility lost to us as children—lost to us as nurses—but regained as the result of professional recovery.

Chapter X Reference Notes

[1]Joani Keller, keynote address at the Annual Conference of the California Association of Nurses in Substance Abuse, June, 1989. Quoting from a paper by Margretta Styles, RN., Ed.D., F.A.A.N.

[2]American Nurses' Association, "Defeating the RCT and Similar Proposals," American Nurses' Association, RCT 4, January 1989, pp. 1-19.

[3]Patrick Carnes, *Out of the Shadows* (Irvine, California: CompCare Publications, Inc., 1986), pp. 54-55.

[4]Anne Wilson Schaef, *Escape From Intimacy* (San Francisco: Harper & Row, 1989).

[5]James Bugental, *Psychotherapy and Process* (Menlo Park, California: Addison-Wesley, 1978), p. 47.

Sow a thought, and you reap an act;
Sow an act, and you reap a habit;
Sow a habit, and you reap a character;
Sow a character, and you reap a destiny.
—Samuel Smiles

XI

PROFESSIONAL RECOVERY: IDEAS FOR ACTION

Support for professional recovery

Many of the following suggestions have emerged from our discussions with nurses and from observing what visionary thinkers in the profession are doing to create hope and possibility for transforming and reempowering nurses. The elements of support for professional recovery are listed in Table 5, page 154. They are discussed in detail below.

Sacred ground

We have said it many times: Professional recovery is supported by personal recovery. If you understand your personal issues and how to work with them, you will be much better equipped to understand how your unique contributions to the nursing profession can be best appreciated and utilized.

From your personal recovery process—and it is a *process*, not an *event*—a dynamic theory of practice emerges. Just as personal recovery is a process of grieving, professional recovery begins with grieving over the losses associated with what nursing has become. We cannot begin to restructure our professional lives until we hurt over the loss of our altruistic fantasies.

Table 5. Elements of a Practice-Based Program of Support for Recovery

Sacred ground (personal recovery)
Evaluating nursing care based on the core issues of codependence
Collaborative governance
Onsite support for recovery
1. Utilization of available resources
2. Nonshaming performance evaluation procedures
3, 4. Pre- and post-shift debriefing in the language of accountability
5. Interdisciplinary forums
6. Affordable childcare
7. Appropriate and adequate financial support for mental health and addiction treatment
8. Onsite therapy conducted by nurse therapists and counselors
9. Annual intervention training
10. Nonshaming recruitment and retention programs
11. Community outreach programs conducted by nurses

Curriculum development
Research
Developing or modifying your theory of practice
Letting go

Simultaneously—and this is the miracle of recovery—hope and new ideas emerge. A renewed sense of possibility springs out of thin air. We become more tolerant, more patient, more capable of moving away from rigidity and perfection, more willing to try new approaches to old problems, more available for self-nurturing, and more appropriate in nurturing our colleagues and patients.

Evaluating nursing care based on the core issues of codependence

To assist professional recovery, we suggest that each health care facility evaluate its policies and procedures in light of the core issues of codependence, asking these questions:

1) Does this policy or procedure support the value of staff members and patients? Is the structure or enforcement of policies or procedures discounting, shaming, or devaluing? If the policy or procedure shames, requires or invites nurses to act shamelessly, or disputes the value of staff members or patients, *change it!*

2) Does this policy or procedure protect and respect the physical, sexual, emotional, and spiritual realities of staff members and patients? If not, *change it!*

3) Does this policy or procedure support the needs and wants of staff members and patients within appropriate, nonshaming parameters? If not, *change it!*

4) Does this policy or procedure accept and support the level of maturity of both staff members and patients without shaming them into conformity? If not, *change it!*

5) Does this policy or procedure promote the accountability and developing spirituality of staff members and patients, or is it rigid, controlled, or unclear? If it denies a nurse or a patient the opportunity to be held accountable for their reality in relation to healing practices or promotes chaos in thinking, feelings, or behavior, *change it!*

At a spiritual level, operating strictly from policies and procedures is banal. Nurse ethicists frequently speak to this dilemma by basing a clinical decision on what is ethical and has integrity, rather than on the letter of the law.

Collaborative governance

Collaborative governance is a concept that comes from the work of Jennifer Jacoby, vice president of nursing services at Roseville Hospital, Roseville, California.[1] It is a unit-based management approach to nursing care that invites participation in management decisions from nurses at all levels.

Differing from other self-governance models, the collaborative-governance model provides simple, clear alternatives to management styles that promote and maintain a more authoritarian approach to patient care. Coupled with onsite support for recovery from issues of codependence, collaborative governance can help to revolutionize management strategies and invite collegial dialogue that is supportive, rather than adversarial, to recovery processes.

Onsite support for recovery

Developing a climate in which recovery can be addressed in the practice place must begin by recognizing that professional recovery is *necessary*. Some insights from our work with addicted families provide useful reminders of what to expect as you develop a program of recovery in the workplace.

Whenever an addict or alcoholic is identified in a family, the family is encouraged to break the "no talk rule." That is, they are supported in the process of getting honest about what living with the disease of addiction has meant to them—physically, emotionally, and spiritually. As they confront the disease and as issues emerge, the minimization, denial, and delusion that have characterized the behavior of every member of the family also emerge. The family frequently is sicker than the addict!

Translating this to the practice setting, you can expect resistance when you suggest to hospital administrators, colleagues, or coworkers that making support groups available to nurses before, during, or after shifts is important to the well-being of the organization. Expect other priorities or plans to take precedence over an administration's willingness to provide funding for a team of nurse therapists to conduct such groups. Much like an alcoholic who denies the impact of her behavior on her family or herself, health care organizations may seem particularly fearful that creating support groups on the premises will have little benefit for nurses.

Onsite support is *necessary*. Ardis Kinney, vice president of patient services; Bill Adamsky, director of the Life Skills Unit; Edyie Brown, education coordinator; and others at Washoe Medical Center, Reno, Nevada, are integrating concepts that bring recovery activities into the workplace with excellent results.[2] The hospital administrators, nurses, and mental health administrators at Washoe have begun shaping a program of professional recovery that incorporates some of the suggestions in this chapter. Education programs, support groups, and policy revisions—all leading to a healthier professional family—have been created despite powerful initial resistance.

Nurse managers, by talking about their own

codependence, make it safe for colleagues to do the same. The "air" feels light in this facility because the heaviness of secrets and fear of shame have been and continue to be confronted. The staff feels valued, heard, acknowledged. Nurses are becoming more creative. Change has occurred and continues to occur as professionals collectively choose recovery. These suggestions work, they make sense, they help.

Creating onsite support involves more than building a new nursing lounge or strengthening the benefit package in some way. Some of the resources for onsite support are already in place and merely need to be utilized. The ingredients of a comprehensive program of professional recovery in the workplace include:

1) Effective utilization of available resources. This includes requesting programs from the nursing education department that place as much importance on the emotional and spiritual development of the staff as they do on refining or developing the staff's clinical expertise. These programs might include such topics as intervention strategy, understanding the issues of codependence, how to support our personal and professional recoveries, professional work with the core issues of codependence, establishing effective personal boundaries, and education on various addictions. Bringing in outside speakers to share their expertise on these issues does more to enhance staff health than an annual stress-reduction seminar, semiannual retreat for selected staff, annual picnic, or Christmas party.

2) Nonshaming performance evaluation procedures. At some level it is crucial to receive feedback about our clinical competence. It also is abso-

lutely necessary to develop and maintain performance evaluation criteria that directly support a nurse's
value, vulnerability, interdependence, level of maturity, accountability, and developing spirituality. To be
truly useful, performance evaluations must be free of
shaming messages, shameless behavior, and carried
feelings—the elements that force conformity through
manipulation and control.

3) Pre-shift debriefing. Before starting each
shift, nurses gather as a group to "check in" with one
another. Doing so addresses each core issue directly.
Taking a few minutes at the beginning of a shift to let
one another know how our day has been prior to
coming to work:

- encourages nurses not to leave their personal issues "at the door";
- lets your colleagues know where your focus
  is (a child up all night with an earache, a
  dying pet, a date with a friend, physical pain,
  emotional pain, joys—the social glue of living); and
- lets your colleagues know where you may
  need support during the shift.

From check-in time at the beginning of a work day,
we:

- have the opportunity to practice asking and
  receiving support for our reality;
- learn to work with our boundaries so we
  don't fix others' pain or take on their responsibility for healing it;
- learn to ask that our needs for time, attention, direction, food, and rest be met in appropriate ways;

- practice living more moderately in an often immoderate work setting; and
- support one another in moving from our positions of perfection and control to accountability and spirituality.

4) Post-shift debriefing. Post-shift debriefing takes another few minutes, gathering as a group to debrief the clinical and nonclinical issues that emerged during the shift. Do this in a structured way, in the language of accountability rather than the language of blame: "When you did or said (insert behavior), I felt (insert feeling)." This gives each of us the opportunity to:

- be held accountable or hold others accountable;
- avoid going home in a pool of anger, resentment, or agitation;
- share appreciation for one another;
- practice receiving praise—something many nurses have a hard time doing because of their low self-esteem.

5) Development of interdisciplinary forums. The goal of these forums is to strengthen dialogue between others on the health care team in light of the issues of codependence. Besides providing helpful information, these forums encourage professional colleagues in other fields to meet with nurses as equals—to speak honestly from their feelings rather than from positions of arrogance, manipulation, and control. Such forums challenge us to do something different.

In one hospital, for example, the mental health team introduced this idea to the administration, then to the medical staff. A day-long seminar followed to explore interdisciplinary recovery issues. From this base, consistent monthly "feelings" meetings have followed, supported by outside speakers. This staff community has become noticeably healthier and has fewer "secrets."

6) Development of a comprehensive, affordable child care program.

7) Development of a benefit package that provides and maintains adequate allowances for mental health benefits, psychotherapy, and addiction treatment not limited to the employing facility. This requires confronting profit margins, the insurance monolith, and financial issues in the health care system. Such financial support requires employers to attend to the emotional, physical, and spiritual health of their staff in more supportive ways.

8) Hiring of both male and female staff psychotherapists or a team of psychotherapists, preferably nurses. These psychotherapists, trained in the management of addiction issues, relapse prevention, and codependence recovery would serve as consultants to staff during worktime, conduct process groups, and provide education and training to nurses on such topics as the nursing role in counseling with patients.

9) Conducting annual staff training on appropriate intervention strategies. Many employers are aware of intervention as a way of assisting individuals into treatment for self-destructive behavior. Most, however, do not use intervention at all, primarily due to a lack of understanding of the process. The single most-reported reason for failing to intervene with colleagues in trouble is fear—particularly fear of legal repercussions. Managed appropriately, there *are* no legal issues.

Thousands of nurses are recovering from addictions in this country. Nurses throughout the United States are gathering support for their personal recoveries from chemical addictions, food addictions, sex addictions, and addictions to other self-defeating behaviors. The price they paid for their dysfunctional behavior finally brought them into a recovery process that saved their lives. Some of them are working recovery programs through state-monitored diversion programs; many are not.

Still others are engaging the fear, shame, and pain of an active addiction that is killing them and creating confusion and chaos in their professional and personal lives. The epilogue from the movie "Deadly Care" noted that one nurse dies daily in the United States from alcoholism alone. Despite what you believe about the origins of addiction, all addictions are treatable. We do our colleagues a tremendous disservice by not approaching them with our concerns about what we see.

If nurses are diverting drugs or coming to work in an altered state due to chemical ingestion, slipping away behind anorexia or bulimia, coming to work with bruises on their arms from beatings at home, unable to ask that needs for rest and food be met, or whiny and unable to function appropriately in the clinical setting, the last thing they need is to be reshamed, swept out the door, or even die because we don't know how to recognize their symptoms or conduct an intervention.

Therefore, we urge employers to conduct regular intervention training programs for nurses and repeat the process annually, much as they do for CPR recertification. Incorporating this technique into the workplace is every bit as powerful as a successful resuscitation effort and probably carries a lower mortality.

Like nursing care planning strategies, intervention with self-defeating behavior is both a process and an event. As a process, intervention provides a simple means of gathering sufficient data and presenting it in loving, nonjudgmental, nonshaming ways, while simultaneously providing an opportunity for help. As an event, intervention is a way of "raising the bottom," creating an opportunity for nurses to get help and remain with a profession that cares about them—rather than reinforcing their self-destructive behavior by addressing it inappropriately or, worse yet, doing nothing. The gift of intervention also allows us to disengage from the self-defeating behavior of colleagues and allows them to take responsibility for their lives—rather than rescuing them, fixing them, or ignoring their pain.

10) Development and support of recruitment and retention programs that appropriately address the substance of true healing through nursing practice rather than creating false, glitzy images. Recruitment strategies must reflect an accurate view of health care realities and must be supported by every licensed nurse in this country. Practicing nurses must believe that their calling to this work and what they have to offer is valued. We believe that work on the issues of codependence will lead to a profound strengthening of the perception of what nursing can become, thus attracting men and women who are truly "called" to nursing work in a deep spiritual sense. The "glitz" will become unnecessary.

11) Development of a community outreach program. This program would carry the message of recovery into the public sector, using nurses who have worked through much of their own personal and professional recovery issues to conduct these programs. Recovering nurses who care about community outreach are wonderful teachers; their skills as educators on these issues have been underutilized inside and outside the workplace.

Extending an invitation to the hospital and institutional committees of Twelve Step groups (Alcoholics Anonymous, Al-Anon, Co-Dependents Anonymous, Alateen, Coda-Teen, Narcotics Anonymous) to bring their meetings into the health care facility on a regular basis would create a bridge to the recovering community. Due to other commitments, nurses frequently are unable to attend meetings as often as their recoveries require. Having meetings available in the workplace provides a solution.

Curriculum development

If we presume that a nurse enters the profession capable of promoting and maintaining health in each of the core issues of codependence, but our experience indicates that this is not the case for more than two-thirds of professional nurses, something is awry. A more synchronistic approach to integrating a man or a woman into the nursing profession would include addressing issues of codependence *in training*.

There is a tremendous amount of information and skill that must be integrated by those aspiring to become nurses. University, college, and hospital training programs are missing a tremendous opportunity to provide the practice place with nurses skilled in the art of living.

Providing didactic and experiential coursework that allows student nurses an opportunity to examine safely their family-of-origin issues while learning nursing skills would incorporate healthier caregivers into the family of nursing. Providing similar experiences and courses for master's and doctoral students is equally important. Continuing to provide support in the practice place through onsite recovery programs would provide a climate for nurses to integrate more effectively their personal and professional recovery activities with their evolving theory of practice.

Further, there would be less disparity between the altruistic ideals of training programs and the day-to-day reality of practice arenas. The benefits for employers, and indeed for the nursing profession, are directly measurable as:

- fewer dollars spent on lost time from work due to stress-related illness or addictions;
- fewer crises stirred up by the misperceived motives of administrations, physicians, nurses, and co workers committed to blaming and shaming rather than accountably promoting health in the organization;
- fewer nurses focused on discounting the stewardship of their colleagues due to the issues of spiritual cynicism;
- greater numbers of patients seeking help from the organization because they have heard or intuitively "know" the organization

"walks its talk" (patients know when the family is healthy); and
• lowered codependence-related morbidity and mortality.

Research

Specific research is needed on issues of addiction and codependence in nursing. Nurses have the capacity to lay the groundwork for profound social, physical, emotional, and spiritual change in this country and throughout the world. Research that develops and tests models of recovery processes in the profession will transform the profession.

• It will focus our energy on a crucial problem.
• It will create a more attractive place for women and men to provide service to others as nurses.
• It will directly address the statistical and hidden shortages in the nursing profession discussed earlier.

Many nurses throughout the United States are aware of—and are developing ways of talking about—codependence and addiction issues in the workplace. "Hitting bottom," whatever that meant for each of them personally, motivated their personal recoveries. "Raising the bottom professionally," through the collective voice of nurses willing to risk lovingly intervening on the profession to promote its recovery, is the goal of this book. We would be irresponsible in writing a book this confrontive without providing useful or hopeful ways of thinking about and planning for the future of nursing. In some ways, we are attempting to conduct an intervention on the nursing profession.

Intervention process in the addiction treatment

profession involves families or groups of concerned persons gathering data to confront lovingly someone they care about who has an addiction problem, while simultaneously providing possibilities for help. Intervention process for the profession of nursing means this:

We invite each of you, the women and men in nursing, to confront lovingly the issues of codependence that affect the practice of nursing at the deepest levels. In this invitation, as with recovery from alcoholism or addiction to drugs, there are no quick fixes. There is, however, a challenge—a challenge to nurses to begin supporting one another instead of continuing to tolerate, promote, and accept the illusions that the disease of codependence invites: abuse, lack of trust, lack of vision.

Developing or modifying your theory of practice

Your theory of practice evolves from your most cherished values in living. Rather than list the theoretical ingredients of nursing as an art or a practice, we invite you, through your own process of clarifying what you believe nursing practice is for you, to think about, feel, and dialogue with your colleagues about your beliefs. Nursing is one of the few professions that allows such latitude in its theoretical views of "what is" in relation to healing.

We suggest you evaluate your theory of practice by answering some questions. Does your theory of practice:

- support your value and the value of others?
- protect your physical, sexual, emotional, and spiritual realities while providing a means

for you to respect and support your colleagues and patients in doing the same?
- promote your interdependence and the interdependence of your colleagues and patients?
- have emotional, physical, and spiritual balance?
- promote your accountability and developing spirituality while accepting and promoting the same in your colleagues and your patients?

Some call it androgyny, some call it yin-yang, others call it "unity consciousness." Whatever *you* call it, this quote from artist Lynn Larsen seems appropriate in relation to an inclusive, unifying theory of practice:

We breath the same air,
We drink the same water,
Begin . . . [3]

Letting go

Just as the personal recovery process shows us how to let go of attachment to our self-defeating behaviors, professional recovery guides us in giving up attachment to whether the nursing profession changes in any way as the result of our awareness and efforts. This does not mean "do nothing." Simply put, "letting go" involves getting out of our own way.

Letting go encourages our willingness to restore power for creating changes within the nursing profession to the forces that guide the unifying consciousness of the universe. Letting go simultaneously brings each of us to a level of personal and professional responsibility that accepts the outcomes.

If we continue to maintain attachment to whether nursing changes, or whether a physician or nurse colleague "gets it," we will stay stuck in the distorted perceptions of codependence, become more resentful of one another, and, paradoxically, compromise the spiritual process of healing ourselves and the profession. As noted before, in early personal recovery, we may begin looking and feeling worse before looking and feeling better. When professional recovery is addressed, the nursing profession undoubtedly will look and feel worse. Remember: Recovery represents the pain of healing, not the pain of rewounding!

The times truly *can* be exciting if we do not practice the rigidity of our disease by resisting ways of talking about and modifying the practice of nursing in light of our collective recoveries. We must turn our attention inward—into our true self, our Child Within—here we will find truth, trust, and the ability to talk from the heart. Here hope and a sense of possibility will provide clarity and substance to our vision.

Begin ...

Chapter XI Reference Notes

[1]For information on collaborative governance, contact Jennifer Jacoby, R.N., M.S., vice president, Nursing Services, Roseville Hospital, 333 Sunrise Ave., Roseville, CA 95661.

[2]For information on bringing recovery activities into the workplace, contact Ardis Kinney, R.N., M.S., vice president, Patient Services, Washoe Medical Center, 77 Pringle Way, Reno, NV 89520.

[3]Lynn Larsen, feminist author and artist, whose painting hangs in our living room.

Love is a hunger;
it is also a skill.
—**Earnie Larsen**

XII

LOVING ONE ANOTHER

Our ability to love and be loved implies a conscious connection between our sense of possibility and the universe. Codependence blocks our knowing, our unity, our capacity to create. Codependence permits us to be confused by paradox, rather than embrace it. But life *is* a paradox. Accepting paradox is accepting two seemingly opposite extremes. Codependence speaks to the pain that paradoxes create; it prevents us from understanding and enjoying the humor in living. Understanding and healing codependence, therefore, returns our sense of humor, our sense of possibility, and our capacity to forgive ourselves and others for living with the disease rather than loving life.

Community—with ourselves, others, the universe—is next to impossible in light of the confusion that codependence creates in us. Loving ourselves and other recovering people as we move through the confusion is exciting, painful, and crucial to our survival. The authors close by sharing our own current progress in recovery. We hope our stories will bring you hope and encouragement.

Candace

This book has been an endeavor in compromise and negotiation between a husband and a wife who have very different styles in almost everything. I felt it was important for each of us to take the opportunity to speak individually about about our codependence, our lives, our recoveries.

My family-of-origin consisted of my mother, father, and younger brother and sister. My father died seven years ago; the rest of my family continues to be a part of my life. We have a rich history, as do most families—one that I won't be writing about. I believe my family has the right to trust that I will protect their privacy until the time that we all are ready to "go public."

My codependence manifested in some classic symptomatology. All of my life I have been most strongly identified with my womanhood and, especially, my mothering. I began mothering children the day a younger sibling came into our home and continued with any child I encountered on through to my own children. I "had a gift," I "loved children," I "was a wonderful mother." All true. I also was codependent and could readily, generously give to others the love that I could not give myself.

In addition to mothering, I became a caregiver to humankind. I was tireless in my availability to hear the problems of others—to help, to fix, to nurture. I embrace this part of me today but no longer "give away" to the extent of abandoning me and *my* need for nurture.

Spiritual cynicism was my deepest sorrow, giving my life a consistent blanket of hopelessness and depression. I learned to mask the pain of it through wit and sarcasm, but lived a life of quiet (and sometimes not so quiet) desperation. I had no idea I could scream out against those messages that kept me trapped in multiple substance addictions and the acceptance of the inappropriate behavior of others.

Today, when that cynicism begins to whisper its despair, I stand and fight. I feel my spiritual power; I feel like a warrior engaged in a battle for my very life. I cannot embrace and celebrate my life with spiritual cynicism in action. This struggle with spiritual cynicism continues to fill me with feelings I find difficult to express.

My mother told me last Christmas that the Storyteller's Creed describes me:

I believe that imagination is stronger than knowledge.

That myth is more potent than history.

That dreams are more powerful than facts.

That hope always triumphs over experience.

That laughter is the only cure for grief.

And I believe that love is stronger than death.[1]

I was so touched by her understanding of me and my way of looking at life, that I cried.

My recovery from codependence is six years old. It began with my efforts, once again, to figure out what was wrong with me and to free myself from depression. With the therapist I chose at that time, I began to work with my Child Within. It was the first real hope I had felt in a long, long time. From then to now, in a nutshell, I have stopped using any mind- or mood-altering substances through a program of recovery; stopped active anorexia and been able to maintain an appropriate weight for height despite crisis, trauma, and stress; and remarried, successfully blending my husband's family with mine. I have done, to the best of my ability, all the things suggested in this book. I have developed a business and have lectured, written, and taught on the subjects of codependence, chemical dependence, and intervention. I have experienced months with a sense of well-being and happiness, with some joy thrown in.

I have been excited, hurt, and angry. I have been passionate in many ways about many things. I have worked every day with my Child Within and have experienced loving myself and accepting myself. As I said to David recently, "If I died right now, it would be all right because I now feel like I have really lived." All of this belongs to recovery and to my Higher Power—I take no credit here. All my best efforts for 38 years couldn't accomplish what six years in recovery has.

As I write this final part of our first book, I'm sitting in a flannel nightgown, drinking chamomile tea, listening to wind chimes on the deck. Could it possibly get better than this?

My hope for each of you is to find this same peace and joy in your lives, your work, your relationships. I pray for a global consciousness and, at the very least, a national consciousness that no longer allows us to abuse any human being and requires of us a sense of community that insists we care for one another. I pray for healing and nurture for each wounded child. And I pray for each parent who, like me, did what they thought was best, discovered it was actually hurtful, and deserves forgiveness of self.

David

There are few issues in this culture that are more difficult for men than recovery from codependence. When I finally had the courage to accept the challenges of self-honesty and look at what I valued in life, I felt the implications of my distorted beliefs about living. Though I spent from 1963 until 1977 in nursing work (as a corpsman in Vietnam, aide, orderly, surgical technician, lab assistant, licensed vocational nurse, respiratory therapist, EEG technician), it was not until I entered the profession of nursing that I felt the challenges created by looking inward.

After I became a registered nurse, I worked as a construction laborer until work in nursing became available at Petaluma Valley Hospital in California. There, I began night work in the newborn nursery. Talk about paradoxes! From carrying lumber, pulling nails, digging in the dirt ... to holding new life in my hands ... I loved both jobs with my whole heart.

Between the time I started work in the nursery and when I entered recovery nearly five years ago, I worked in emergency departments and critical care units, attended a year of medical school, taught clinical nursing, and accumulated enough certifying initials after my name to more than qualify as one who gathers esteem from the outside in.

Within three months of sobriety, I was working as a staff nurse in an addiction treatment facility. I was out to sober up the world and tell everyone how wonderful I was, until I was dropped to my knees by codependence. I was alone, angry, filled with fear and shame, and wanted to pin responsibility for my pain on anyone but myself. I had used alcohol and other chemicals, sex, work, spending money, exercise, food, sugar, caffeine, and other things to sedate my pain—quickly changing from one to another whenever I sensed someone was getting too close and might find out I was sick. I "looked" good (or so I thought) but felt soul-sick.

I came to nursing without my own thinking (using research or others' ideas as my own), feeling ashamed of thoughts I had about healing, and fearful, believing I didn't have the right to speak up or out. Unaware of my neediness, I was able to use the theories of others and take care of others to shore myself up. I excelled, and my colleagues fed me the definition of myself that I created for them. I never felt full.

When lecturing to nurses about codependence, I have been accused of projecting my own stuff onto them or sharing the soap opera of my marital life. At the other extreme, nurse colleagues have said my work has provided significant healing for them or has been the most powerful seminar they have attended in 22 years of nursing. I am comfortable with both extremes, since today, as a result of recovery, what you see of me is what you get. I also believe that most people will not trust a colleague who stands before them challenging them to change their behavior, if they sense the speaker's words don't match his or her own behavior.

Healing my codependence has been very hard for me. I came into recovery arrogant, walled, needless, supernurse, perfectionistic, and controlled. While I was training with Pia Mellody to teach others, she said, "You can't become self-esteeming, protective

and respectful, interdependent, balanced, accountable, and spiritual until you feel the pain of your
disease." I hated her for months!

I can only tell you, that by working consistently
with my Child Within and making a commitment to
stay in one place while listening to his teachings, I
have moved in recovery. I also have been lovingly
cared for by friends, my wife and children, and my
Higher Power.

When I slip into the delusion that I have coau-
thored a book filled with personal bias that does not
apply to anyone but me, I have only to listen to other
women and men in nursing who tell me the truth
about myself and the profession. I know this work has
value. Today, because of recovery, I also have a sense
of my own value that protects me from a shame attack
if I hear that this book may not apply to you. Like
Candace, I apply all of the principles in this book to my
life. And while I do this quite imperfectly, the principles work for me and for my relationships. I pray
they will be useful to you in your life and work.

Our first national lecture began at the invitation
of a friend living and working with the poor in the
Adams-Morgan district of Washington, D.C. Not
since my public health nursing experience in Berkeley,
California, while training to become a nurse, had I
been so jarred. My life as a husband, father, son,
brother, friend, teacher, and nurse keeps bringing me
back, through paradox, to the poor. I am given this
gift by my profession—the fellowship of nursing—
that sustains me as I heal and helps me live!

I wrote the following four years ago as part of an

address to graduating nursing students. I had a shame attack and could not read it then. It fits here:

Invocation for Nursing

We find nurses with the blind, with the criminally insane, in alternative birth centers, in one-room cabins in Appalachia, in office practices, in acute care and skilled nursing facilities with the latest in technologies, in homes with the dying, in inner city barrios and side street clinics with the poor, in schools counseling a child in pain, in addiction recovery facilities where fear, anger, pain, and shame are turned from enemies into teachers. We find nurses with a thousand different cultures and people with skins of many hues. The scenarios are all different.

Though each of us is on our own journey in search of our own truth, the spiritual energy in us all is the same. That spiritual energy fills the heart of a mother who lives with her four children in a van behind a 24-hour market. That spiritual energy sustains the life of a South African father spooning a slurry of rice water into the mouth of his dying son.

We are joined in acknowledging this truth by no mere coincidence. We are joined in this place to lift our hearts, our hope, and our capacity to grieve, to love, to forgive, and to heal, by the light of the ancestral spirit ... that on their journeys into healing, the women and men in nursing may sustain themselves in their call— that they may live in faith and know that no matter what Truth they embrace as their own, healing is an affair of the heart.

Chapter XII Reference Note

[1]Storyteller's Creed taken from the introduction to Robert Fulgham, *All I Really Needed to Know I Learned in Kindergarten* (New York: Villard Books, 1986).

RESOURCE LIST

This is a partial list of resources that may help you in recovery. We do not endorse one program, organization, or book over another. Recovery is like a trip to a new place. Rather than reading someone else's account of their journey, use these resources to create your own.

TWELVE STEP SELF-HELP PROGRAMS

Each of these programs offers help through the experience, strength, and hope shared by their members. They are not affiliated with any religious group or organization. The only requirement for membership is a desire to heal. The offices listed below can give you information on chapters in your area.

ALCOHOLICS ANONYMOUS WORLD SERVICES (AA)
P.O. Box 459
Grand Central Station
New York, NY 10016
(212) 686-1100

ALANON FAMILY GROUPS HEADQUARTERS (Al-Anon)
(Help for family members and friends of alcoholics)
P.O. Box 862
Midtown Station
New York, NY 10018-0862
(212) 302-7240

ALATEEN
(Help for teens with alcoholic family members or friends)
P.O. Box 862
Midtown Station
New York, NY 10018-0862
(212) 302-7240

COCAINE ANONYMOUS WORLD SERVICES, INC.
P.O. Box 1367
Culver City, CA 90232
(213) 559-5833

CO-DEPENDENTS ANONYMOUS (CoDA)
P.O. Box 33577
Phoenix, AZ 85067-3577
(602) 277-7991

CODA-TEEN
(Help for teens with family or personal issues of codependence)
P.O. Box 33577
Phoenix, AZ 85067-3577
(602) 277-7991

CO-DEPENDENTS ANONYMOUS FOR HEALTH PROFES-
SIONALS (CoDAHP)
P.O. Box 18191
Mesa, AZ 85212
(602) 971-3284

GAMBLERS ANONYMOUS (GA)
International Service Office
P.O. Box 17173
Los Angeles, CA 90017
(213) 386-8789

INTERNATIONAL NURSES ANONYMOUS (INA)
(Support for nurses in recovery who are working other Twelve
Step programs)
(415) 386-3014

NARANON FAMILY GROUPS (NarAnon)
(Help for family members and friends of drug addicts)
World Service Headquarters, Inc.
P.O. Box 2562
Palos Verdes Peninsula, CA 90274
(213) 547-5800

NARCOTICS ANONYMOUS WORLD SERVICES (NA)
P.O. Box 9999
Van Nuys, CA 91409
(818) 780-3951

OVEREATERS ANONYMOUS WORLD SERVICE OFFICE
(OA)
P.O. Box 92870
Los Angeles, CA 90009
(213) 542-8363

SEX ADDICTS ANONYMOUS (SAA)
P.O. Box 3038
Minneapolis, MN 55403
(612) 339-0217

CO-SEX ADDICTS ANONYMOUS (CoSA)
P.O. Box 14537
Minneapolis, MN 55414

SEX AND LOVE ADDICTS ANONYMOUS (SLAA)
P.O. Box 119 New Town Branch
Boston, MA 02258
(617) 332-1845

S-ANON FAMILY GROUPS (S-Anon)
(Help for those dealing with family members' or friends' sexual
addiction)
(818) 990-6910

SMOKERS ANONYMOUS (SA)
World Service Office
2118 Greenwich St.
San Francisco, CA 94123
(415) 922-8575

OTHER RESOURCES

AMERICAN NURSES' ASSOCIATION (ANA)
2424 Pershing Road
Kansas City, MO 64108
(816) 474-5720

COCAINE HOTLINE, INFORMATION AND REFERRAL
1-800-COCAINE

NATIONAL ASSOCIATION OF ALCOHOL & DRUG ABUSE
COUNSELORS (NAADAC)
3717 Columbia Pike, Suite 300
Arlington, VA 22204
(703) 720-4644

NATIONAL CONSORTIUM OF CHEMICAL DEPENDENCY
NURSES (NCCDN)
975 Oak Street, Suite 675
Eugene, OR 97401
1-800-87NCCDN

NATIONAL COUNCIL ON COMPULSIVE GAMBLING (NCCG)
445 West 59th Street
New York, NY 10019
1-800-522-4700

NATIONAL COUNCIL ON ALCOHOLISM (NCA)
12 West 21st Street
7th Floor
New York, NY 10010
(212) 206-6700

NATIONAL CLEARINGHOUSE FOR ALCOHOL INFORMA-
TION
(An excellent resource for computer-researched data on addic-
tions, the Clearinghouse is a service of the National Institute on
Alcohol Abuse and Alcoholism.)
P.O. Box 2345
Rockville, MD 20852
(301) 468-2600

NATIONAL INTERVENTION REFERRAL NETWORK
(619) 693-1433

NATIONAL NURSES SOCIETY ON ADDICTIONS (NNSA)
2506 Gross Point Road
Evanston, IL 60201
(312) 475-7300

SUGGESTED READING

Addictions

Leaving The Enchanted Forest: The Path From Relationship Addiction to Intimacy. Liana Becket and Stephanie Covington

Chemical Dependency in Nursing. LeClair Bissell, Eleanor Sullivan, and Etta Williams

Treating the Alcoholic: A Developmental Model of Recovery. Stephanie Brown

Straight Talk About Drinking: Teenagers Speak Out About Alcohol. Wayne Coffey

The Chemical Brain: The Neurochemistry of Addictive Disorders. Sidney Cohen

Shopaholics: Serious Help for Addicted Spenders. Janet E. Damon

Women and Drugs: Getting Hooked, Getting Clean. Emanuel Peluso and Lucy Silvay Peluso

Getting Better Inside Alcoholics Anonymous. Nan Robertson

The Addictive Organization. Anne Wilson Schaef

When Society Becomes An Addict. Anne Wilson Schaef

Alcoholism, Attachments, and Spirituality: A Transpersonal Approach. Charles Whitfield

Adult Children

It Will Never Happen To Me. Claudia Black

Repeat After Me. Claudia Black

Treating Adult Children of Alcoholics. Stephanie Brown

A Time To Heal: The Road to Recovery For Adult Children of Alcoholics. Timmen Cermak

I Should Be Happy. Why Do I Hurt? Earnie Larsen

Old Patterns, New Truths: Beyond the Adult Child Syndrome. Earnie Larsen

Hope: New Choices and Recovery Strategies for Adult Children of Alcoholics. Emily Marlin

Adult Children of Alcoholics. Janet G. Woititz

Codependence

Abused No More. Robert J. Ackerman and Susan E. Pickering

Beyond Codependency: And Getting Better All the Time. Melody Beattie

Codependent No More. Melody Beattie

Diagnosing and Treating Codependence. Timmen Cermak
Facing Codependence. Pia Mellody
Do I Have To Give Up Me To Be Loved By You? Jordan Paul and
   Margaret Paul
Codependence:Misunderstood—Mistreated. Anne Wilson Schaef
Escape From Intimacy. Anne Wilson Schaef
Lost in the Shuffle: The Codependent Reality. Robert Subby
Codependence (formerly published as *Codependence: An Emerg-
   ing Issue*). Sharon Wegscheider-Cruse, Ed.
Healing The Child Within. Charles Whitfield
A Gift To Myself. Charles Whitfield

Eating Disorders
*Feeding The Empty Heart: Adult Children and Compulsive
   Eating.* Tyeis Baker-Baumann and Barbara McFarland
Surviving An Eating Disorder. Judith Brisman, Michele Siegel,
   and Margot Weinshel
Fat Is A Family Affair. Judy Hollis

Family
Black Families in Therapy. Nancy Boyd-Franklin
Bradshaw On: The Family. John Bradshaw
The History of Childhood: The Untold Story of Child Abuse.
   Lloyd de Mause, Ed.
The Hero Within: Six Archetypes We Live By. Carol Pearson
Not My Family: Sharing The Truth About Alcoholism. Maine B.
   Rosenberg, Ed.
*Before It's Too Late: Working With Substance Abuse in the
   Family.* David Treadway

Intervention
Intervention With Helping Professionals. Linda Bailey and
   LeClair Bissell
Living On The Edge. G.L. Gustafson and Katherine Ketcham
Intervention: How To Help Someone Who Doesn't Want Help.
   Vernon Johnson
Beginning Of A Miracle. M. David Meagher
Freeing Someone You Know From Alcohol And Other Drugs.
   Chandler Scott McMillan And Ronald L. Rogers
Crisis Intervention. Ed Storti

Sexual Abuse and Sex Addiction

Out of the Shadows. Patrick Carnes

Looking For Love In All the Wrong Places. Jed Diamond

The Right To Innocence: Healing The Trauma Of Childhood Sexual Abuse. Beverly Engel

Triumph Over Darkness: Understanding And Healing The Trauma of Childhood Sexual Abuse. Leslie Hatton and Wendy Wood

Victims No Longer. (Men recovering from incest and other childhood sexual abuse.) Mike Lew

Shame

Healing the Shame That Binds You. John Bradshaw

Facing Shame. Merle Fossum and Marilyn Mason

Shame: The Power of Caring. Gershen Kaufman

Spirituality

Spiritual Choices. Dick Anthony, Bruce Ecker, and Ken Wilbur

Healing the Body, Mending the Mind. Joan Boryschenko

Days of Healing, Days of Joy. Carol Larsen Hegerty and Earnie Larsen

Healing The Wounds: A Physician Looks At His Work. David Hilfiker

Out of Darkness Into The Light. Gerald Jampolsky

Beyond Addiction. Lee Jampolsky

The Quiet Answer. Hugh Prather

Love, Medicine, and Miracles. Bernie Siegel

Peace, Love, and Healing. Bernie Siegel

ABOUT THE AUTHORS

Candace Snow and David Willard, R.N., C.D., C.A.C., bring over 26 years in the helping professions to their work as educators and consultants for those interested in healing from the diseases of addiction and family system dysfunction.

Snow and Willard are wife and husband, and partners in Past Company, an education, training, and consulting firm that provides assistance through private consultation, seminars, and staff training. Their clients include individuals, groups, employers, school systems, health care providers, and addiction treatment providers. Past Company provides services on issues related to addictions, intervention, codependence, and program design and development.

Snow and Willard have lectured throughout the United States and England, and are adjunct faculty for the alcohol and drug studies programs at Chapman College and the University of California, Santa Cruz.

For more information, contact the authors at:
Past Company
27820 Dorris Drive, Suite 201
Carmel, CA 93923
(408) 626-2656

Professional Counselor Books is a division of A/D Communications Corporation

A/D Communications Corporation is a communications firm dedicated to educating people about addictions. Currently the company is achieving this through the following:

Professional Counselor Magazine serves professionals working in the addictions field.

Adolescent Counselor Magazine is for anyone interested in learning more about adolescents and addictions.

Professional Addictions Training produces and sponsors seminars and conferences on a variety of subjects, all dealing with addictions. (Sponsor of the annual National Adolescent Addictions Conference.)

Professional Counselor Films educates people on addictions through films and videos featuring professionals from the field.

Professional Counselor Books produces quality books on a variety of subjects focusing on "wellness."

For information write:
A/D Communications Corporation
P.O. Box 2079
Redmond, WA 98073-2079
or call
1-800-622-7762
206-867-5024 (In Washington State)

A book of light-hearted humor for adult children of alcoholics and adult children of trauma. This cartoon book pokes fun at the many unspoken facts, truths, myths, and coping mechanisms of growing up in a dysfunctional family. It is intended to help support persons who have experienced the pain of rejection, loneliness, sadness, shame, guilt, and isolation by adding a touch of humor to an otherwise bleak situation. It is also designed to encourage individuals to laugh at themselves and realize, in such a tough spot, that "I am not alone."

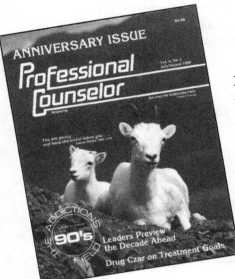